PALABRAS LUMINOSAS (Luminous Words):
The Alternative New Year's Day Spoken Word / Performance Extravaganza
- 2016 Anthology

- First Edition.
- Volume III in a series.
- 152 pages.
- Trade Paperback.
- American contemporary poetry anthology.

Contact Information / Order Online:
http://www.alternativenyd.org/

Rogue Scholars Press
http://www.roguescholars.com

Design and Layout: C. D. Johnson
Publishers: Rogue Scholasr Press
Front Cover / Frontispiece: "Luminous Words" (with 'Apollo And Diana'
by Albrecht Dürer)

ISBN-10: 0-9840982-3-2
ISBN-13: 978-0-9840982-3-1

Published by Rogue Scholars Press
New York, NY - USA

PALABRAS LUMINOSAS

Luminous Words

**The Alternative
New Year's Day
Spoken Word / Performance
Extravaganza!**

2016 Anthology

http://alternativenyd.org

CONTENTS

CONTENTS Continued...

II

CONTENTS Continued...

APPENDIX

ACKNOWLEDGMENTS

It is terrific that the the Alternative New Year's Day Spoken Word / Performance Extravaganza is being accompanied for the third year in a row with an anthology celebrating the writing of many of the featured performers. Every year we attempt to freshen up the event by adding a substantial new group of performers and reaching out to different areas of the tri-state area. For the last two years Thaddeus Rutkowski has played a principal role in working with a group of outside curators who have their pulse on emerging as well as more established talents, who then bring some of these people into our fold. Once part of our mix we often reach out to them in future years to come back and join us. This year the group of outside curators has included Gabriel Don, Russ Green, Wayne Kral, Jane Ormerod and Vittoria Repetto.

When I began this event in 1995 at Café Nico on Avenue A between East 6th and 7th streets our staff was small, and I was responsible for most of the effort (Larry Jones, Joanne Pagano, John Holt, and Grace Period were other key players). Now we have a wonderful staff who help with myriad aspects of the event, from scheduling the clockers to writing the first draft of the press release to reaching out to outside curators as Thad has done to broaden and expand our mix. In addition to Thad, key staff members this year have included Madeline Artenberg, Boni Joi, Ptr Kozlowski, Annmarie Lockhart, Ellen Aug Lytle, Su Polo, Robert Roth, my wife [now] Joanne Pagano Weber, Merissa Anderson who volunteered her time this year as assistant editor, Miriam Stanley for her continued support of Rogue Scholars Press, and of course C. D. Johnson, who has produced this wonderful anthology and designed our logo, flyer and poster. Thanks C. D. – you are a gem. Finally, we would like to thank the management of the Nuyorican Poets Café who have welcomed us since 2014 when this anthology first took flight.

- Bruce Weber

The annual event, which has taken place every New Year's Day since 1995, was founded by poet and art historian Bruce Weber and quickly became one of the most popular events on the city's poetry scene. Mr. Weber returns to oversee this year's production after a one-year hiatus, ably assisted by a staff of poets, writers and designers. "This is an amazing contingent of performers rocking all day and into the night from all sides of the city and beyond — lots of fresh voices and new discoveries," Mr. Weber said.

The Alternative New Year's Day Spoken Word / Performance Extravaganza features poets, monologists, musicians, dancers and other performers in a 10-hour showcase of some of New York's most talented writers and artists. The lineup that evolves each year to keep the event as fresh and democratic as possible.

Collected here in this volume is just a fraction of the talented voices brought to bear every New Year's Day in New York's East village. This anthology is the next best thing to being there. If you sniff the pages, you can actually smell the poets. Smells like wine, ink, and existential crisis.

Austin Alexis

Policing

Some cops care about order
but not the law.
Some cops smell of silver
wafting from their sweaty badges,
or from their heated metal bullets.
Ask a kid yanked from her school seat
by a manic officer
what odor he carried on him,
along with his club and handcuffs,
as he lurched toward her
that smoldering afternoon.
She might say he gave off
a whiff of fear
or even terror,
not of her
but of The Establishment
he (rightly or wrongly) felt behind him,
prodding him with a broomstick.

Joel Allegretti

The Man Who Slept 23 Hours A Day

spent his 60 conscious minutes bathing,
eating a meal, reading newspaper headlines
and preparing for the next cycle of sleep.
As he approached his 80th year
and heard death humming in his bones,
he realized he had done nothing
by which the world could remember him.

His clock winding down, he embarked
on an ambitious course of achievement.

He created a symphony with one note,
an epic poem with one word,
a novel with one sentence,
a drama with a single line of dialogue,
a self-portrait with a brush stroke,
a sculpture with one strike of the chisel,
a mathematical formula with one number.

When he died he was acclaimed for a life
of accomplishment and versatility.

Amber

Snow Pea

Snow Pea is a pod with newly developing peas
It is eaten whole while the pod is unripe
From the French <u>mange tout</u>, eat all.
Perhaps the snow comes from a whitish tint emanating from the
pod
But peeing in the snow, writing your name in the snow, will
produce yellow snow
That's the snow you don't want to <u>mange tout</u>
Is it true that no snowflake matches any other?
Snow is hard or soft, big or small, dry or wet, slushy and mushy,
shiny or gray
Or sparkles and glints in the cold night moon light
A special wintry array
Snow peas can be giant, mammoth, melting or dwarf
Snow balls are fun or a very aggressive form of interaction.
With a pea at its center, the ball can be very hard
The abominable snow person, parts composed of ice, climbs over
the mountain top
Skiing down with excellent form.
Braving brutal, harsh, rigid icy winter storms
The sleigh of the ice queen flies on the surface.
Snow peas enhance salads, soups, spring rolls and stir-fries
Raw, raw, raw in its greatest flavoring.
At the end of the winter snow, the young delicate shoot pokes its
head up
It is crisp and tender and tastes of green
Support this dainty, delicious immature legume
As you support the early budding and continuing development of
peace
A plan hatched during the winter isolation
Peas, peace, peas, peace, peace please
Peace can be green and dainty and very tasty, <u>mange tout</u>

Maria Aponte

Passing Thoughts

How desperately we cling to the past.

Places and times captured in grainy black and white photographs,
a time when right was right, wrong was wrong,
even though the right was wrong and the wrong was right.
The years that passed brought modernity and liberation,
free speeches and free sex and diversity,
changing skin colors a sign of changing times.
The years that passed awakened and educated,
but did they enlighten?
Today, everyone is demanding attention.
The We / Us is now I.
The I puts past moral and values on the shelf:
"That was good for back then, but not now."
Forgetting, then is now.

Except, the now is metal and plastic, PCs and cell phones,
Game Boys, Play Stations, and I Pods,
High fat processed food,
empty calories to fill empty souls,
a bottomless pit of hunger for garbage
approved by sold out corporations
hiding behind their familiar guises:
"It's good for you."
"It'll make you feel better."
"Try it, you'll like it!"
We've bought the hype, believed the hype,
sold it to our children, who are full of answers
without understanding the question.

We say we have so much to offer. Offer what? Offer whom?
We either over-intellectualize or over-analyze.
We've "been there, done that!"
Our consequences are "Whatever!"
When the sun graces us with its light,
we say, "It's about time!"
instead of, Thank You.

(From Transitions of a Nuyorican Cinderella)

Madeline Artenberg

Conversation With Father

Under the palms in the parking lot
behind your condo, I'm complaining
how mother still drives me nuts.
You follow with the litany,
"She nags every hair on my head,
counts every breath,
she's going to kill me."
I ask why you stay.
This time, instead of shrugging,
you tell me, "I would've left years ago –
I couldn't -- we didn't do that in those days.
It's too late now."

Your words carve the air
as your name will do a few months later
on your headstone.

Mother still says she tried her best.
Did you ever notice the other women
looking at you, Daddy,
with warm-gloved eyes?

Ayres

I Am a Flim-Maker (Sic)!

The woman @ WALGREENS of indeterminate Asian origin [(Korean or Chinese. There is a difference. Usually, I can tell, have (had) enough experience, been around (them) enough (to know). But, in this instance, can't (for some reason)]. She's fooled me. Probably, Chinese? Though, Koreans can go either way. Says "Flim" (sic) instead of "film," like a lot of Asians (do) who mispronounce (their) words, or get it backwards. This is (fairly) common. "You make a lot of flim (sic)," she says. "Every day," I tell her." You must be a flim-maker (sic)," she says. "Yeah. Lady, every day, I make flim (sic)," I respond. The woman @ WALGREENS thinks I work in Hollywood [Why is it: When(ever) I tell people I make movies, they assume this? This is why I'd rather not.) Could it be wishful thinking (on their part)? They don't realize: There's a whole world or (other) worlds (levels) of film–making (going on) out here & that I exist on the bottom or lowest rung, on purpose, &, maybe, like it that way, never occurs to them.] Immediately, her eyes light up. She sees dollar signs, I can tell. To her, this is what I represent (money). But, everything is relative, right? &, to her, &, where she's from, maybe, possibly, I am wealthy! (Add to that) the fact (that) I am able to shoot film, or, her word, "flim" (sic) at all! Maybe, she is right? I am rich! … But she's not used to people complaining about Kodak. Wanting to send their pictures back. … The woman @ WALGREENS (who) says: "Flim" (sic) instead of "film." …

Carmen Bardeguez–Brown

Conjugations

We are verbs searching for meaning
In the vast ocean of existence.

You
I
We
Us

Intertwine in hibiscus and roses
Amapolas
And
Flamboyan

We are shadows of love
Burned in the ashes of sorrow.

Us
We
You
I

Dance in circles
Smelling earth and corpses.

We are love awaiting to feel.
We are pain
Forgiving to cry.

And
You
I
We
Us
Are

crystals
Capullos congelados
Encrypted
Quietly
Murmuring
For the door of wisdom
To open our heart.

Gabriella M. Belfiglio

Grace

Around the table,
home-made wine is poured and passed.
Children whine with delicious need.
In a singular moment of silence,
my aunt asks if anyone wants to say grace.
I think of my cousin
whose bulging left calf
displays a large inked cross,
or my godmother
who has a tiny gold
one around her pink neck,
or my girlfriend who was forced to church
every Sunday of her childhood,
or my brother who has found God
as an adult and reads
his Bible everyday like practicing
the stretch of octaves on his piano.
Surprising myself, I immediately offer.
I thank my Aunt Marie, for hosting us—
all in two parallel tables crammed into her cozy dinning room—
I thank everyone present,
for being so, I thank the farmers for the food,
and I stop after I quickly extol
the universe itself.
I don't mention God.
My grandmother, sitting a few folding chairs to my left,
who's approaching one hundred, softly comments:
I always thanked the farmers too
remembering a different decade.
I'm overcome with love for her and this gravid family she's
created.
Some of us have died.
Some have been in prison.
Some have fought in wars.
Some of us have protested war in front of the White House.
Some of us have physically attacked others at the table.
Some have physically attacked themselves.
Some of us have PhDs and some never finished high school.

Some of us have not been able to stay out of rehab.
Some sneak cigarettes and convince themselves no one will notice
their smoky breath when they kiss goodbye. Some have just
started talking.
Some have said things they regret.
Some of us judge some of us without ever saying a word.
All of us have forgiven someone here for something
we have now forgotten. With a chorus
of *salute*, glasses click into a crescendo of chaos.

Jennifer Blowdryer

Never Explain Never Apologize

Rage is good
but without ruthlessness
it is a loser emotion
get those teeth fixed

Patricia Carragon

Lost Weekend Via The Coney Island Bound D Train
(For David Francis)

Pre-Halloween track work—
The MTA's "Lost Weekend" journey.
The D train to Coney Island,
an N train in drag.

A slo-mo freak show
behind smeared plexiglass.
Shanties moon the banks
of the puke-green creek.
In garbage dump forests,
trees of heaven
strip in sunlight.
Can-crushed cars
in assorted positions—
an orgy of Skittles' color.
Grungy trash
does the "full monty"
on crabgrass.
Nature falls in love
with graffiti sludge.

"Life is beautiful,"
a clichéd haiku meltdown—
"enjoy the journey."

Tina Chan

The In-Between Girl

The In-Between Girl
Rebound
When men claim the standard: "We are on a break"
How men use me as the in-between girl
Fill the temporary void
The after-thought
The missing link
Taste tester
Space holder
Seat warmer
The alternate
The back seat
Contingency plan
The third party
Plan B
Back-up girl
Test drive

The In-Between Girl
Why do you put me in limbo?
If you don't like my package do yourself a favor: do not open it!
Don't break bread with me if you don't have any sincere desire for
me
The outlook remains murky
Look deeper within me
I ain't your hollaback girl!
Can you sincerely accept me to be your long-term girl?
Do not use me to burn bridges, do you understand?!
I am so much more than what you see on the outside

Steve Dalachinsky

For Hersch

the space vacated the ear oh the air i meant you the heartpump
of survival the greatness of a love supreme generosities the share
the lion's share of sharing meeting in small space radio
bewitchment
you saw me thru my words indeed & it seemed our friendship
like a movement in history always was even before our birth &
so we fill the space which we evacuate reside in it ourselves
resident aliens for the brief time known as life time – the act of
honesty an act for others this business of friendship the dignity
you possess
this complete truth is your wealth not like ½ truth & ½ truth =
#@?
but ONE big YOU no compromise

i mean you systematic springtime eternal staple state of the art
guy
flippy trippy simply grand your hands your lifeline's heaven on
earth
angel eyes a jazzy rap beyond this crazy quilt of spontaneity
am i gettin' thru these obscure images we share in our non-
conformist
sweet tooth lives oh precious candy store man this solo's all for
You
the best & on the right path without the vanity of shining
& so you shine like no other in this cockeyed balancing act this
allegory
of faith in the great big IT the poetry of the void & annoyed
stark naked starlit starfish that you are father poet friend

MENTSCH

in this CITY CITY CITY.

Vivian Demuth

The Age Of Extinction

A few nights ago, a bear danced around
my garden carrots and bowed to sniff
the sow's scat in the soil bed.
Last summer, a deer yanked my Tibetan prayer flags
from fire-tower scaffolding and paraded adorned
antlers past trampled skulls in the broken forest.
I am a human animal walking a dirt trail of illusions
tossing vegetable scraps a mile from fire-tower
cabin for the closest or quickest to snack.
In my first six years of fire-lookout solitude wrestling
I saw a hungry caribou outrun a wild six-pack
of dart-gun helicopters,
heard ravens chuckle circling above loggers'
orange flagging tape alit in forest flames,
followed a scarred moose chase a fleeing Honda generator
along another new mountain road,
and took photos of a wolf pack stealing the seismic
camp's grilling steaks and biting off a page
from the First Handbook of Habitat Protection.
Over the next six years from mountain heights,
I've watched the wildlife thin and the oil
drills strike back.
Is this the Age of Extinction in which only Fortune's
wheels will roll on?
I pray that some drugged grizzly will wake up
and flip the switch.
Can a human ever gain the insight of a drugged bear?
In the meantime, I'll sit in the petrified bedrock
with what looks like a young dinosaur
and write for the unwritten record.

Pete Dolack

The Magic Of The Market Comes To A National Park Near You

The yuppie couple in the tent next door
Bring in their take-out pizza
Despite all the warnings against keeping food after dark
That's good
Because if the bears come
They'll attack their tent and not mine
Though the bears ought to get paid for making an appearance
Since this is a for-profit park
I don't know what the government would do
If Yosemite stopped being profitable
One concessionaire already controls everything in the park
Would it be allowed to foreclose?
Maybe this is the first step in privatizing the parks
And then it'll be made so expensive to visit
That only yuppies and the rich will be able to stay there
We'll sneak into the park disguised as rangers
Then plant food inside the tents to draw out the bears
Putting new meaning into the concept of "eat the rich"
But too much of this will get the bears fired
No one will have civil service protection
Once the parks are fully privatized
Certainly not the bears
It would be a sad sight to see bears in the unemployment office
With few options
They might wind up in the military
Hopelessly out of their element in the desert
Unless this is seen as an acclimation program for the bears
Under full privatization
Parks will reach their full profit potential
All the hunting licenses that can be sold would be sold
The trees cut down
Until the parks are reduced to desert
And now the bears can come home
When their tours of duty in the desert are finished
Because they will now be acclimated for the parks
But with nothing left but barren ground

And a few disgruntled bears
Who are hungry too because there is nothing left to scavenge
The land will be of no use except as target practice for the military
And the bears will already be used to bombs dropping
A new way to see the nation
Bomb Yosemite! Bomb Yellowstone! Bomb Arcadia!
The psychological benefits of parks bombing will be
immeasurable
If you can bomb your own parks
Bombing other countries will be even easier
Making it easier to export these ideals
More humanitarian bombing
Will lead to new privatized governments elsewhere
Which will sell bombing rights to their parks cheaper
Enabling the military to cancel its national parks leases
There will finally be no more profits to be made
The private parks company will sell the parks
Back to the government
They will again be open to all
Which will be fine by the rich
Since they won't be interested in traveling to a wasteland
And the newly admitted will plant a tree

Gabriel Don

August 4th 2015

"To think we did all that and not in a shy way."

The mother was late
"denial"
but when she arrived
her and an entourage dressed in black
crowded and cuddled at the coffin
and her mother fiddled with her daughter's
hair and redid her make up
and repositioned the flower
a few times
before removing it.
Her mother asked me who I was, "Friend? Friend?"
I nodded yes, didn't say, "Lover."

Akeem K. Duncan

When We Thought We'd Live Forever

It was me, her...

The bobby soxers. The attaboys.

We smoked jazz cigarettes and took pictures,
hoping that somehow it would last longer than it was supposed to
but it never did.

The future was cruel, knocking us down one by one...

I saw Ruth just the other day. She's still a looker but only I and
those who are left ever had the pleasure of witnessing her in the
prime of her pulchritude.

Her soft skin glowed as if she had the sun on a leash.
Her eyes beamed, a no nonsense glare that could cut a man in
half.
Her breasts swayed gently every time she made a gesture with her
hands...

which was often.

We once slept together during the summer,
after a night of gallery hopping, whiskey and dumplings.

We stumbled home glued at the hip. Giggling and singing
"Mercedes Benz" so loud, the dark windows above became lit and
populated with aggravated shadows.

She would later tell me in the following winter, hiding her blushing
cheeks behind an oversized mug of cocoa,

"It was the way you held me that night, all the way home, you held
me. Even when I'd let go, you held me. I was drunk... but it meant
something. It meant a lot.

And you weren't sweaty.
You're always sweaty. [Laughs]"

We remained closed, cuddling in between relationships but never pushing the boundaries of our own.

She has a family now, a neglectful husband and an eight year-old daughter she loves to bits.

She no longer finds time to stumble with me. But whenever we see one another in passing, we hug a little longer than we should, as if to say,

"I miss you
and somewhere in time we're still stumbling,
hip to hip,
never letting go."

Bill Evans

Beastie Girls

Arriving with our band
Beastie Girls
To compete for
The prize on
American Idol

Neither girls, exactly
Nor beasts, yet
Ferociously
Sensitive
On television, no less

And all for
Big poetry dollars!
Glory, surely
Just kidding
Either love us or get rid of us

All for naught
I mean Art, superlative
Radiant energy
Bounce to the moon
And back again

No doubt, for *song*

Very busy missing
Us once we're gone
You can take
My word for it
Transitional, transformational, transactional, transcendental

Transcontinental, transmogrificational...

Yet forgiving everyone
Gathering the pieces
Relentlessly, patiently
By eye and hand, by ear
And heart, by the book, by hook *and* crook

By yes, no, and maybe, in between the lines
In the name of we told you so
In the name of get off your ass and get going

And don't look back, for the Furies are behind!

What's gone is done
For better or worse
In sickness and in health

Until death do us part

Cheryl J. Fish

Stand Clear Of The Closing Doors

If there's loss take to the real
Home is a bone deep breath

Windswept sounds of where
It's the people before time

Their voices touch you
alone blue flying, no crime
Make some.

Sleeping notion. Hand in face
Focus soft cut
End open

Before time
people
Fly
Making blue soft crime

Try to sleep. Face in the morning
Windswept.

Bryan Fox

Secrets

permeate the walls of
Bronx tenements. It's what lies beneath floral
patterns and family
matters. When a young lady sits
at the dinner table, she is to close
her legs, it's no laughing
matter. My mother said, "hand
shakes only, no high fives when you are talking
to men." "You need to be lady
like, you're not supposed to be talking
to men." The shame I felt was live, because in many Latino
families the truth
is being a women is synonymous with being
useless. She is
dirty, she is
unworthy, so I learned quickly
how to keep
a secret. Keep my mouth how I keep my legs
closed. If I dare
come out of my face, I got slapped
in my face. "She is to be seen, not
heard." I need to be prim and
proper, as delicate as these
secrets, like monsters in disguise as
angels on wall paper. The ones in the family
you would never imagine
would cut you soul
deep, while touching you
so deep, till my soul like Swiss
cheese. That God sized hole
I need to fill so I eat
my grandmothers rice and
beans, along with my self
pity.

Luis H. Francia

The Flounders Of Evil

You could tell. They were hell-bent on trouble, their ride pure swagger, their fish-eye stares pentecostal, daring you to hook them, gills itching to go great guns. Lean and mean, they swam in from Flanders, from Florida, from the country the Spanish call Francia.

In the day's boulangerie, they were the sour cream of the crop. Mention the word "fry" and they would get steamed. Mention rapscallion, though not scallion, and these stalwarts of the deep would wiggle their fins in pleasure. No flounderers, these. Their spines stiff, their sleek heads filled with thoughts of their founding fathers, well-read in their breviary, their scales bore the weight of vigilante justice, ready to fillet and fry you in your fat.

Hook, line, and sinker.

Armando Jaramillo Garcia

How Much I Love This Now

Two summers followed by winter
Approaching the landing in line
The horizon extending its hand to the eye
Two dozen eggs breaking in the mind
Saying simply this is only for pleasure
And the sounds that expose the struts
Say you now know the burden is double
Two springs followed by fall
Clean and dress the wounds
You worked hard to acquire
Which began to feel like plenty
Though in essence you are somewhat poor
Say the windows are blackened for better sleep
That builds a mountain out of a few sticks
There you can climb in your rough clothes
Where two winters followed no weather at all

Robert Gibbons

The Violence Of A Sexual Act

Oh gilded silver face, not so easy to escape the violence, not so easy to say am not going to bother with all of this stabilimenta, the heavy zigzagging, cracks open the newspaper or the web, how to frame an aurantia, how to name it orb-weaver, or carnivorous predator the orange or yellow markings, the bruised black in back grounds the attraction in search of a potential mate.

so she waits in her one frame house, her one chance for marriage regardless of consequence, the barriers to the media-infused carrier, her abdomen is an egg-shape before the one year termination, but he Is not the aggravating husband, he co-mingles as planned, the writer should be like her, the biter
the fighter.

this is violence, she kills him in print, in their short stint reunion, who is at fault with her three claws per foot, her fingernails use to spin sticky silk makes her hub a death bed, takes on items twice her size so he dies from a compromised immune system.

Russ Green

Poker Face

I learned to play poker in a dim
lit basement by a guy with cashback
eyes. There were women there who
were hotter than habaneras on a bed
of burning chili sprouts. There was
one in particular with bright red bra
straps hugging her angular too smooth
fuck me thin shoulders who couldn't
hold a poker face to save her own lover's
life once her temperature started to rise. I
had three of a kind and aces high. We were
all high. No, not that kinda high. I mean
we were high on each other. The sweat poured
while the fan roared. There was nothin' any
one of us could do but hang onto this blood
boilin' rocket propelled moment barreling
straight through the center of our most personal
and sinful confessional booth admissions.
These were actions that would make rosary
beads bleed in the hands of the Pope on Fifth
Avenue. I mean royal flushed faces lit up the
previously impenetrable darkness beyond those
curious windows and shined all the way to Venus!
We let the milky way have its way in its own
classic milky way. We were ridin' that bad boy
wave right into the thin sleeves of that switchback
of razor sharp dreams. We had messages from
the eternal goddesses of pesto promises and pickled
radish renditions of Satchmo songs on our side.
We showed the backside of those cards the upside
of paradise in a sky high shake shack that shimmered
every time its name got mentioned.

Antonia Greenberg

Soddom And Gimorrah

An angel
Fingers covered in pizza grease
A cigarette hanging between her lips
Fingers prying
Your tongue from behind your clenched teeth
A receipt tucked into her denim jacket pocket: sporting condom
wrappers and trident gum

The brass clock overhead reminding us
it's nearly noon again!
All the scared little people rush inside the church
Scurrying past us with tiny feet leaving tiny prints pressed into the
heaving pavement
she might've walked you from Broadway to 116th

Salvation something like clutching a purple feathered hat to your
breast
And a bible… Pages dissolve readily between your fingers
Smelling of pizza grease
And a smile played out upon her thin lips covered in pink gloss

As she tells you none of it was ever divine
her jacket zipper caught in her ruffled wing
That sex was just sex
The aftermath: a lull in a voracious appetite.. A cease fire in a war
against passion.
You called it something of a resolution. Hallelujah.
pulsing, throbbing, as she lent you a corner of her heaven in the
bathroom of a Pizza Hut
Her feet interlocked with yours

Peering at scraps of newspaper taped into a book
With purple duct tape
Placed high on a linoleum shelf
Of places and faces smeared with fingerprints

You might call it unfamiliar
Had you not seen them all written across her stony features
As someone plucked the strings to an invisible harp in her mind
And she shed a single brass tear
For pizza grease
And time forgotten by the deli counter

Jane B. Grenier

A Diamond I Be

On my souls journey past the dark side of the moon of blue,
the red road freed me
to be me.
To see.
Once a queen forever a queen.
Yesterday we lived for tomorrow,
tomorrow we live for today.
Enraptured by beauty,
I would rather be a butterfly
in a shadowless wasteland of soulful sorrows...
Dancing with myself.
The Bliss of Love upon me...
Carrying sunshine in my pocket...
Dreaming eternal dreams through soul searching eyes...
Gathering memories from fields of flowers...
In this world of tender mercies
blinding fears cloud my vision.
To cry a little and then I smile.
Through the haze of dark I see...
A sparkling diamond I be.

Bob Heman

Acts Of Innuendo

the begins the room
this closing the wall
as tall a word there
as could so arrange

they left hatchways
under the commas
and lived there waiting
to exclaim a distance

explaining only
each word there as
a shadow or some part
of the required extent

and there had tied it
so they could be pulled
inside or across it and
waiting to be meant

the lines churning the flesh
where they entered or
where they were deflected
by new acts of innuendo

Aimee Herman

Kind Of Like Citrus

I didn't understand why you needed to pay me; you had jesus christ abdominal muscles and all your hair. You were young enough to remind me that you hadn't married yet but think about proposing to your girlfriend who lives long distance.

You told me my hair was pretty and I was pretty but not like your girlfriend is pretty; she is beautiful, you said.

All your furniture matched and you had fancy pillows on your bed and I wondered how long-distance this girlfriend really was. I only saw you that one time and I can still remember that your semen tasted expensive. Like your tan. Like citrus.

Roxanne Hoffman

Make A Wish Or What I Want For Christmas
(For John "Jack" Edward Cooper)

how we retrofit our lives:
penciling plans;
rescheduling schedules;
clocks set back, we spring forward,
take this leap of faith —
reality suspended midair —
and like children
waiting for Santa's delivery,
we hug, locking in embrace,
eyes closed tight,
our dreams pouring forth
like clover's amber-hued honey
from lust-loosed tongues;
we buzz like bees,
as the snow drifts down,
glitter before street lamps
against the black-drop of night,
hushing all around us —
pure and white,
the flakes — now the size of moths;
eyelashes fluttering,
hearts ticking away from any boundary of time,
we talk and talk and talk,
pollinating most perfect memories.

David Huberman

Straight Outta Thailand

I knew their was trouble when I got to Bangkok airport. It usually takes twenty minutes to go through customs, if even that. So when it turned into a hour and half waiting game I could tell something was up. I was pretty worn out by then. I had been prodded onto a line where I had to deal with a older female Thai national custom agent with a perpetual frown on her face. Exhausted and pissed off I wanted to tell her that there are no direct flights from New York to Bangkok anymore. The only way was to take a flight through China, either Beijing or Shanghai, that's a fourteen to sixteen hour flight. Then on my four hour layover, you don't fall a sleep because Shanghai is very cold in November and their hotels are not very cheap. Then you got to go through Chinese customs which is no joke (Don't be coughing in front of those people ! You never know where you can end up--organ donor time ! American passport-- we don't know where he went ? Humbug !) So I'm on the flight to Bangkok and that's another five hours. Did I mention that I also went through American customs ? They didn't care for my after shave balm, took two of them away, but they let me keep my medicated hemorrhoidal relief pads. Win some, lose some as they say. Well by now readers you must realize that I love Thailand ! But back to the older female Thai custom agent with the perpetual frown, so now I'm finally in front of her. She inspecting my passport and I figure we'll another two minutes, Bangkok I have arrived ! But she says " where are your papers ? " I say, " what papers ? " With a nasty look that could kill, she says " how did you get to Bangkok airport ? " I'm gone, for a few seconds. I don't comprehend, then I slowly say " I went through Shanghai. " " Good, now lets see your airline tickets." Her frown is becoming a perpetual sneer by now. She hates me and I hate her just as much. In fifteen years of going back and forth to Thailand I have never been asked for connecting airline tickets. I usually throw them away, but thank God I didn't do it this time. It takes me a while but I find them and hand them over to her. She takes a good look and then says " For now on have all your papers ready. Go now ! " I was so spent, it kept me from acting out in anger. I wanted to tell her she's a bitch from hell. I'm glad that I didn't, because I would have been totally wrong. The lady was only doing her job. I knew there was a terrorist attack in Bangkok a month ago in a Hindu temple, what I didn't know was another bomb went off this past week. After I left the airport behind, I entered a ghost town. I went to my favorite province of Thailand, Pattaya Beach and the other tourists were no where to be seen. The local expats that I knew from just hanging around over the years were three ex IRA guys, they gave me warm hellos but their mood changed rapidly. They told me " Mr. Huberman we know your ways, don't go to favorite night club, you like the young women (late twenties to early thirties) the terrorists are targeting the young now, the Insomnia club could be their next example to made by them, god help us all ! " They walked away scared and paranoid or maybe they weren't. All I know right now is my modern life resembles that apocalyptic, futuristic film "Brazil ". The end for now(hopefully).

Kate Irving

I Dreamed Something About To Happen

Trash cans rattle
Antennas twitch with signal
Electric air bites into lungs
Dead sparrows feet straight up
Heads are being oiled teeth pulled
Someone's about to be catapulted
Judges sit in judgement
Dogs howl in the squares
The sun rising in the west
The sky swims in a black sea
Men call down from high floors
Singing to the sound of small artillery
Streets are burning
Flaming oil is falling rain
The children are silent
The children

Evie Ivy

Even Pathways

Because of the avenue where joy takes place
time tries to keep all in balanced order.
No wind must sweep incautious through streets,
places and roads. Peace belongs to all who seek it.

We need the masquerade. There must be
temples for redemption in every route
where the soul must find itself again.

We can't all live in the Avenue of Joy.
Yet each story has its beginning and end,
with surprise jumping at every character in life's
living page—where dread can always circle on.

We need the avenue where joy resides
to balance and remind us that when good comes,
be there for it. We've seen shells of what once

was laid here and there—with sadness we move
over. We need the avenue where joy takes hold,
all evens out and good things come to flow
into every street and avenue, place and road.

C. D. Johnson

Doll Lies Broken On The Sidewalk

Doll lies broken on the sidewalk,
Matted yellow hair tied in a worn scarf,
Dirty face, dirty fingers,
Runny nose.

Beige beholden lips,
Hide and seek tongue,
Rose chin, translucent skin,
Hard-grey sapient eyes.

Deep cut on otherwise flawless cheek,
Slender neck and back, spine protruding in detail,
Loose filthy pink tank-top shirt with anarchist A,
Nothing beneath.

Pale yellow twine rope belt,
Light gray jeans, aged significantly to dark gray,
Ripped in inappropriate areas
Around thighs and groin.

Sockless brown ankles,
Black sneakers...
Converse...
Chuck Taylor...in perfect mint condition.

"Yo, Bro, can I bum a cigarette?" – she asks.
"I don't smoke." – I reply.
"Bummer." – she says.

"Can I get a buck or two?" – she asks.
"For cigarettes?" – I ask.
"No. I'm pretty hungry." – she says.

I reach into my pocket,
Finding her a five dollar bill.

I hand it down to her.

She takes it between her fingers,
Rising up off of the pavement.

"Thank you, friend." – she says.

A sudden kiss on the left side of my face,
And then she's walking away.

Boni Joi

Application Profile

I begin a poem with objects
That feel safe from the outside

I observe the outside and collage over the rest
Forget spiders in my brain that move around at night

I'm on a nightly news strike but can't avoid advertising
I used to be a young girl but now I'm a plastic bottle

Plastic bottles can be recycled into t-shirts and other useful items
Like drones that can be operated from the other side of the world

I refuse to drone on about my familiar feeling of agitation and
Instead follow the trail of old gum to the next super-sale

The sales-line at the pharmacy is short
For people with optical character recognition

My mother was an inconsistent character with a nice smile
In her last manic episode she was a children's songbook

I didn't pretend to be operational just episodically challenged
For peace of mind I jogged over junkies in East River Park

Now I clean up messy web junk and reformat my feelings to
        fit the screen
There's a Swiss Alp for flashes of clarity

The flashes of a lighthouse in the dark spaces
Where the ocean of the mind goes blank.

43

Tobi Joi

The Smell Of The World

1

Kid Gordon was apprentice to
the lord who knew just what to do
but then he saw the evil ones
people were slowly turning to

So it was time to break away
take what he learned & take it away
now he fights to save the world
Kid Gordon knows that it will be worth it

2

I wish to be the chosen one
that leads the world to a better time
and if you think I'm not able to
please push me I will come through

Chorus I

What can we do
　　　　to reverse the pollution?
What can we do?
　　　　We can't put it on the moon
You got it in your nose
　　　　the smell of the world
Would it be perfumed?
　　　　The smell of the world

3

I wish to be a super human being
fly around destroy every weapon
would save oil for good use
have a little time to repair the ozone
Every human being is so guilty
of somehow everything mad in the world
O my O my it's such a pity
that no one else see's that it could be pretty

4

I wish to be a super human being
fly around destroy every weapon
to make the company man understand
super power is everyone

Chorus II

What can we do
            to reverse the pollution?
What can we do?
            We can't put it on the moon
People slow down
            Kid Gordon solution
Everybody's down
            for the green revolution.

Larry Jones

first evening star

*...the long bar of maroontint away / solitary by itself...**

across a copper bar
a penny for your thoughts
upon first evening star

Sunday evening from afar
first of few brilliant dots
across a copper bar

club *Paraiso del mar*
the night lures and plots
upon first evening star

who would play to par
across all life's noughts
across a copper bar

an hour away by car
a kindly crowd of soughts
upon first evening star

the sea's refrain *del mar*
a penny for your thoughts
across a copper bar
upon first eastern star

*"There Was A Child Went Forth," Walt Whitman

Meg Kaizu

Undercurrent

I break shells & make us sunny-side up eggs
      Smell of coffee & butter
         I hum smiling

           Solar eclipse outside my window
      Darkness drips & paints the pane of glass black
I can't see out, I hear a fight next door

They're shouting
Something clatters
Breaks on the floor

I shut the blinds
"Stop! Stop! Stop!" I scream & cover my ears

      Eat my eggs, drink my coffee, just as sand absorbs blood

         This land is full & plenty, as sweet & cosmetic as
frosting

           The landscape, background, undercurrent

"It says suicide," you say & put down my story.
      "That's not true. It was a homicide," I reply.

      Rocks, stones, pebbles, sand, dust

      You throw my work on the desk, curse, "Stop writing
bullshit".
"It's not bullshit," I say.

On the walls, in the streets, graffiti
      Everywhere I stroll, the sky is hazy
         As opaque and slimy as egg & sperm

Ron Kolm

My Name Is Dexter

I make a decent living
Selling insurance
To worried newlyweds.
After work
I sit in a neighborhood bar
And watch the sports
On TV.

My friends tell me
I complicate my life
By always meeting
The wrong kind of women --
But really
I'm just a simple guy.

I love to follow
The crazy twinkling lights
As they streak across
The evening sky
And I stand on the sidewalk
Quite still
Bathed by the moon.

Ptr Kozlowski

Where's My Poem?

Where's my poem?
I'm supposed to have one.
Why don't I?
What happened to it?
Why isn't it here?
I don't even have a tracking number.
I've got plenty of nuthin'
but nuthin's not plenty for me.
I'm supposed to have something –
some bring-something-to-the-table type of thing.
some self-expression to actualize,
some pent-up rant to purge.
some felicitous sequencing of syllabic content.
Where is it?
People say, write about what you know –
but I don't know –
can I really write about "Hot Enough For You?"
and "How Are the Roads?" and "Have a Nice Day",
"No Problem", and "Have a Good Weekend"?
"Thanks", "OK Thanks", "Thanks a Lot" and "No Thanks"?
"What's Up?" "What's New?"
"Not too bad and how are you"?
"Would you like an apple pie with your order? Today?"
Where's my poem?
How come I don't have one !!?

Wayne Kral

LESwindowSHOPPING

When I drink and am enlightened
Watching one foot behind the other
Knowing home is around any corner
Passing banks, boutique money covers
Chain stores, why bother?
Snub my nose at your dis-order
Sitting next to dinosaurs
Windows covered, gates down
Mindful of anarchist robbers
Mindful of your hate for the left-overs
I miss Lenny for what he said
I miss Barbara because she's dead
I miss Mick before he danced with Taylor Swift
I want to break your window
But I gotta buy a brick

Jane LeCroy

Prize

It's not true
that the one who dies
with the most money wins
Bend at your knees
so they can't look up your dress
Draw on fake eyebrows and feel gorgeous,
they'll believe in you
Repetition convinces everyone;
that's how religion succeeded
Sneeze in the crook of your arm
so you don't spread germs
Let your wild eyebrows connect and feel sexy,
it shall be true
Everyone knows a smoker who lived to 93,
the prize is the game
You can't figure it out and nothing is fair
Everyone knows
a non-smoker who died of cancer young
If you choose the Kaiser roll
that's been sitting next to the donuts
it tastes like a donut
Paint doesn't fix things,
it just makes them look better
Whitewash the hours with near misses
and you hit the mark
Pain doesn't enhance things,
it just makes them meaningful
The target is bigger than it looks
and you're better than you think
The end is stuck to the beginning,
it never helps to isolate them
Whoever dies with the most tricks
up their ripped apart sleeves,
that's who wins
No need to compete

Linda Lerner

The Road Back To Yemen From A Brooklyn Laundromat Goes Up In Smoke

separate, he asks, as he puts my laundry
on the scale. Yes, *separate*, I say
still...week after week, tries to make
this American woman understand
what it feels like, no, make me smell
the smoke of mortar & rocket fire politics
keeping him from getting his wife & daughter
everything so carefully arranged, end of
June, his graduation from college, and then...*puff*
do you see?
                        what I see is the road
twisting and turning in his mind
teasing him *now it's here, now it's gone*
of a promised cease fire;

when he speaks of his birth country
of things getting worse
I see frightened people imprisoned
in their homes being deprived of basic necessities

I see a country being raped...
I do not see his wife and daughter
he will not let me

(This poem was published in New Verse News on 11 / 12 / 2015)
and was nominated for a Pushcart Prize)

Phillip X Levine

Philquips

we wouldn't write if we weren't consumed
and driven by the total and utter fear that
we had nothing, absolutely and completely
nothing to say
*

There's a history of mental illness in my family.
Probably a future too.
*

seeking partner who will overlook my neediness,
desperation, banality, shallowness, transparency,
pettiness, smallness, and overall mediocrity and
accept me for what i truly am
*

i'm so distracted
i can't even focus on my obsessions
*

have you seen the Good News Bible?
he doesn't die in the end
*

i've never had a fatal accident
*

meeting new people is like
arriving in the middle of a movie
except you're allowed to talk
*

i knew she was psychic
from the moment she told me
*

Welcome to Woodstock
Gateway to... uh

Steven T. Licardi

Hot Track Blues

"I shall pass this way but once."
Oh no, my darling,
I've ridden this route before,
seen the way this island changes over
miles and miles.
A flip book
of overcrowded stick-figures,
jostling for space on this sandbar
drifting out to sea.
Ours is a concrete cancer
that can't seem to stay inside the margins.
I have seen the way the sun rises
over steel beams and papier-mâché.
Looking glasses
that make it *so hard* to look away.
I witnessed you standing
in the cleavage of Lady Liberty,
smooshed between the ample breasts
of 5th Avenue
and Macdougal Street.
My ears tell me
there is a five-alarm fire burning
down the block from where we kissed
and it's moments like this that make me wish
we weren't capable of longing.
This city is slowly sinking,
arteries clogged with traffic jams,
taxi cabs lodged in capillaries.
This city
is dying
of cardiovascular disease.
You can taste it in Times Square,
but here
on the LIRR,
all I can think about
between Penn Station and Babylon
is where it is you're lying.
Is it warm?

Is it gentle?
Is it safe?
Is he certain?
Is he prepared to take the plunge
like that sad city you're steeped in?
that sad city you're steeped in?
The breadcrumbs you've been leaving
have fed the sewer rats for months,
while only subway tunnels know
how deep my love for you runs.
This city never sleeps,
but is hardly ever kept up making love.
I hope you are.
I *dread* that you are.
I've ridden this branch a thousand times before.
To dine on acrylic,
woodcut, armor,
plastic, oil, ink.
Now I wander,
a part of me hoping our paths will meet,
while another fears
I will wind up
at your door.

Tsaurah Litzky

Last Tango

After seeing "Talk to Me, Marlon" at the Film Forum
I know I've always been in love with Marlon Brando,
how many times have I replayed his films in my mind,
his voice alone brings me to ecstasy.

In Streetcar I cast myself as Stella, though actually in
temperament I'm closer to Blanche,
in Last Tango I play Jeanne the young Parisienne,
speaking bad French with my Brooklyn accent,
we embrace, his hand hot on my back,
he leads with his left foot, he prances, I sway,
we promenade, our passions escalate,
our bodies do a mad fandango,
as long as I am with him, I am young and beautiful.

Could he be the God of Wishes Granted,
wearing his bald spot for a wreath on his head...

The film said he had twenty children,
then he is shown speaking to the press,
devastated, after the suicide of his daughter Cheyanne,
old and fat as he has become, I still love him.

On the street, after the movie, I'm not young and beautiful,
anymore, men don't turn to look at me as I pass,
I don't care, in my heart I dance with Marlon Brando,
he holds me fast.

Veronica Liu

Night Court Nights

Last night I watched maybe three and a half episodes on tape before I fell asleep on the couch (and awoke to a clip of the final round of a Jeopardy episode where Harry Anderson was playing— and winning). The first and second episodes were the two-parter during which Roz finds out she has diabetes and Dan pretends to be her father so he can talk her down from the ledge of the roof with an imaginary mocha fudge ice cream after he spends most of the episode directing lewd jokes toward Roz's doctor. I remember reading some uproar from viewers long ago who were distraught at the portrayal of people with diabetes. Okay. The other plot running through this show is that it's the 200th anniversary of the US Constitution, and besides the nationally televised show-stopping finger-popping constitutional blowout bash that is going down, some guy is holding hostage one of the original drafts of the Constitution so he can eventually buy 30 seconds of Judge Harry's time to tell him that everyone is technically supposed to be equal. Best line, paraphrased: Bull: I tried to get her down from the salad bar but she kicked me in the... cafeteria. The third episode I watched was the one where Art asks the non-mulleted Christine to go to the Buffalo Lodge Banquet, and Christine attends out of pity, plays piano, inadvertently insults Art after being harassed by others all night, then they both have a moment in the courtroom after it is all over. I do appreciate the climactic turn when Art claims he didn't really want to take Christine anyway. The last episode I watched before dozing off featured, my favourite and yours, Buddy Ryan, who moves out of his digs at the institution because they get rid of the square dancing, and, after discovering that his pal Norbie's place is only in his mind, moves in with Harry. Father-son tension and reconciliation ensue. European flight attendants are involved. Christine gets the haircut she sports for many of the later seasons. In the Jeopardy clip, Harry is in the lead with $14,000 but screws up the last question; category: comedians. Gerald Ford told this person, "You're a very funny suburb." Harry guesses Louie Anderson, saying he was going for size, but opponent Sinbad poses the correct question: "Who is Chevy Chase?"

Ellen Aug Lytle

We Can All Live Better Thru Electricity

who says the apple tree outside
the bathroom window, hasn't
got a glass slipper

in europe i'm higher than you

i can look down from a 2nd story, see
you relaxed in a shady park
there's a dog, a yellow toy
clutched in his paw

but a different year
spain smells like tobacco:
maja perfume and field hands
chatting under hammocked trees

we sleep near her border in my sunbeam alpine
2 toddlers in the jump seat, our dog then,
a cocker, gypsy, stays in switzerland
w / jacques and mme seveso

and barcelona, middle class, sweaty,
me 20, pregnant for the 3rd time, checked
into a hotel w / a dumbwaiter hoisting wheat
up, down, past our room, trapping me between

sky high trees that monitor dark boulevards
and a prayer to help w / something fearful
perversely, injections from him:
'this will make you bleed,
                    or not'

fall is coming
bread and jam on the table, not
just green trees stalking a white sky
but summer's bulge before the explosion
we can all live better thru electricity

Nancy Mercado

The Wife

I have always heard of monsters
have read about them in fables and stories

I never really believed in monsters
never thought I'd come across one in my waking life
until I met you

You are the essence of what a monster would be for me
Uncaring
abrasive
selfish
devoid of compassion

You're claws and green scales hidden within you

Marlene Nadle

Eisenhower Snapshot (12 / 31 / 59)

Mamie wears mauve for New Years. Her full taffeta skirt rustles as she moves across the chintz-filled living room of the Eisenhower cottage, tucked away under the trees of the Augusta National Golf Club. Dutifully, she clusters with the other wives wearing matching white orchid corsages.

The buffet is set with black-eyed peas for luck. It is an old Georgia tradition. So is the segregation that lingers at the club that was once a plantation. The only Negroes present night, or any night, are servants. The President brought his own Negro. John attended him in the army and is busy putting more platters of ham on the table.

Eisenhower sports the green jacket of a club member. His bald, pink head is tilted back in laughter. He even enjoys the doggerel verses about his presidency written and read aloud by the Chairman of Coca-Cola.

At midnight they toast with champagne. The glasses are lifted high by the wealthy men surrounding Ike, all swathed in Augusta Green like Robin Hood's merry band, only in reverse.

Uche Nduka

The Matter

he sings a tune. he smudges a tune.
i walk in the night
then i listen to flowers.
warm enough under a spell
the need the feast in being naked.
a kind of dance we might have danced.
a kind of waterwheel. a kind of watergourd.
the white silk talks about God.
i quarrel with tedium.
what i am given is both rabbinical & libidinal.
the whole egg–tempera thing.
tenderness born of exile.
luminous with sex
you glide by twice.
pines tell tales about us.
hot night too hot to touch.
nor is there room
for the price of laughter.
a green flute
hands a baton to a white violin.
sob stories on the shelves.
a half loaf of light.
for the flagstones had been neglected
but not the foresails.
& the shaft of loose living & beauty & breasts.
plaited blue on either side.
& took up one side of the sky
while we went sea–weeding.
the space love demands.
go full navel but don't
make me say Pretend you're writing poetry.
living life
sourcing the silver bridge
something got said got said.
keep contempt at bay, stay vital,
praise the borderless day.

Ngoma

The Magazine Cover Said Is Beyoncé Pregnant?

WTF
Who gives a rats ass
surely not me
She can afford it
Im trying to figure out
Where all the people moved
that were displaced by the Barclay Center
or what the rich can do to end world hunger
I mean really
there's so much other stuff to ponder
like what the hell happened to 200 girls in Nigeria
Some say it didn't happen
conspiracy theorist
scream it's a psyop
That the Taliban,Isis and Alquaida are all manufactured
to keep the gun factories employed
as we sacrifice blood for oil
Hell why should it matter to me if Beyoncé has another baby
I'm sure it's nothing she can't handle
Meanwhile y'all be wondering
what's gonna happen next on Scandal
I want to know why seasons are out of season
and if world war 3 is on the horizon
I want to know the reason
I'm looking for solutions
to atmosphere pollution
or away to eliminate child prostitution
now that so called slavery is done
can we get reparations
these magazines just want to increase sales
I'm trying to find a way to keep young Black Men out of jails
and really who cares about
Is Beyonce pregnant...
REALLY?

Bri Onishea

Christmas Spirits

Coat the world in downy-frost, a cold tickle of winter
layering the earth in six-pointed stars fallen from heaven.

There are things I still don't believe: not beyond
what I can   touch   taste   whisper   hear

see. Hills and valleys bundled, an open invitation
for wipe-outs and sleds, days spent

forgetting our fingers and toes, our bodies
slowly transforming into snow

men, no trace yet of the ice monsters building inside us.

We were always refugees, huddled against your soaking coat
at the base of the hill as you prepared to lead us

downward into battle. There was no guarantee we'd return
with all our mittens or teeth. I remember

we were always where we shouldn't be:
an abandoned school, an historic cemetery—

is it sacrilege to play among the dead? Or do you think they envy
us our laughter, our too-red cheeked, cherry-nosed fun?

I sometimes snuck out after we arrived
safely home, to share lukewarm chocolate with the spirits who

lingered on our back porch.
I felt in them nostalgia, a child's imagination

seeking to fill in the gaps between constellations—

I do not believe in what is beyond my senses,

but I sensed them. Stories and memories strung
like ornaments, some glass-crafted and delicate;

others old and wooden, hand-painted. Snowflakes like souls,
fingerprinted with generations.

Jane Ormerod

Pitfall

This is the life of the world of the had to, the ever-needy retching strong. This is the life of the rat flatterer, a statistic of dinner as usual, a mutual misunderstanding that isn't standing because there is no standing, and the pain of lying, sleeping, eating, beeping, and touch, touch, and touch. Because the first line is help, the funny of improvement, and hope, and hospital corridors that look like canals of the dead.

Go deeper—these are disused corridors. A shortcut from ward to wrong street. The sold dog, the biggest dog, the dog the cause not the child. The shortcut has an angle, a few more dresses that aren't dresses but are stubborn, but are smart, but are tiles, are dragons, are broken, are instant and knowing. A lot of little pretties. Pretties on own time and a word and an insistent friend. The time is 5:50 pm, there is no more water, just flat hands with instruction, the fifty million wheels, the geography of ink and this is the geography that she can't see. The geography of movement, a table that welcomes, a woman eating shoes on a filthy Sunday.

Play pretty, play fluffball, swingball, play with spaghetti bolognese. Remember the water, the hat, the queen, the unnecessary baby, the elbow back when it was simply elbow, the water when it was water. Remember the lighthouse, the speed that never was, horizontal light, the never touch, the flinch and linen, and water and say respectable not respect.

Learn to be difficult. Do as you are not told. Become continental. Forget the reason why you were made into you.

Leila Ortiz

Forever Lonely

It's been too long
since the sky was
a dance floor.

Who knew
growing up meant
nothing's ever

the same. Jelly sandals
with Minnie on the buckle.
How the smell of wet

woods or a barbecue
in a city park can make me
small again.

Later I wore a name plate.
Forever Lonely—
thick gold around my neck,

my boyfriend's jeans
pegged at the ankle.
Baby powder,

his smell. A voice
came through a screen
as we watched

videos after school.
His old sofa, his carpeted
floor, the velvet fear
of sex.

Yuko Otomo

Moment
(For Herschel Silverman)

A moment lives in a moment, the past, the present & the future

Small palms quietly set on the train window
crossing the continent
he saw everything / nothing-ness of life
shine in a vast landscape
under the bright / dark american sky
when he was a boy
way before "they" hit the road

A moment breathes in a moment, the past, the present & the future

Rubbing his hard-working hands reflectively
casting a glance toward his equally hard-working loving wife
while getting the sunday papers ready for the early morning
customers
in a pre-dawn winter air
scooping ice cream & making the perfect egg cream
for kids after school, his own & the others' in summer
in a city of wide boulevards
a man of genuine beatitude lived the life of a poet & a father
in a total wholesomeness
while "they" were overblowing their somewhat artificial images
in spotlights, here & abroad

A moment proves a moment, the past, the present & the future

Standing on his belief of creation & poesy
he recites his work with an honest passion
on a stage big or small
sharing the moment with anyone who listens
to show us ways in a golden eternity
to be music
to see ourselves clearly
to be naturally who we originally are

To be humble is "beat", JK said –
who can be more truly "beat" than who once helped "the beats" in
need?

A moment celebrates a moment, the past, the present & the future

Thank you, Hersch, a friend, a teacher of Life

Amy Ouzoonian

November 23rd

Phoenix sunrise stirs ASU grads from smokey sleep
To their sandwich artist jobs at Jimmy John's.

Downstairs from the dude hive,
Far from christmas lit doorways
Boyfriends walk their girlfriends to cars
Their faces slowly unraveling
Into a zero humidity morning.

A caravan of millenials are barreling in
Celebrating the victory of making it
Home alive.

One stops and asks if I have a light
For his cigarette.
He's wearing a t-shirt that says
Mid-life Crisis.

They're one of his fav bands
They played at the Crescent last night
The show was poppin'
Only one guy was arrested
A Mexican
From Nogales
They're hoping he makes it out
For Thanksgiving.

Eve Packer

today: 11 / 19 / 15: &

how can i get past
bombs placed in
planes espresso
wine sippers
having, or not,
a cigarette--
eviscerated
      by AK-47's,
students &
popcorn munchers
shredded blown
apart for the crime
of waking up
alive--

oh, if only--
humans had
one, a shard, a fraction
of a single
angel wing--

Mireya Perez

Everything You Need To Know About The 5th Grade

She knew that the vision would come on the corner elm tree
because
she was so good in
school she heard that Our Lady came to the three children of
Fatima
and that St. Ignatius
fell wounded then found the Lord and was saved and that St.
Genevieve
saved the city of
Paris from that barbarian Attila and that St. Lucy gave her life for
her faith and they took
her eyes so why couldn't she have the vision too so she stared at
the tree 'til her eyes
teared and when she entered the church she kissed the ground
because
maybe the vision
would come then maybe the statue of Our Lady would come to life
so she
always made
sure her shoes were shined and her navy uniform skirt and white
blouse
immaculate and
her nails short and clean and her ears washed because she wanted
to be
ready for the
vision and in classes at St. Bart's the white habits of the
Dominicans swished through the aisles fast as the sisters drilled
her in grammar, spelling, math (short and long division) and the
exercises to focus on the stories of the saints like the martyrdom
of Joan of Arc who was just 14 and a warrior and savior of her
nation maybe that's why she wasn't interested in playing jump
rope but would walk around with the sister on duty so she could
catch a glimpse of the elm tree

Puma Perl

Another Memory

Bob Hart was known
to throw his poems away
after a reading
I pretend to do the same
But I cheat
Crumple them up
onstage
in a dramatic gesture
Or comedic
Later I gather
the poems
like leaves
on sidewalks
Dirty
Creased
Stepped on
Stuff them in my pocket
for future use

What good are they?

Elegant of word
Shiny black pen
Long legged lines
Solitary dances

This morning
Bicycles flew silently
up the FDR

The wind woke me

I remade the bed
meticulously,
returned to dream
of car batteries
stolen,
air conditioners,
off brand vodka
dinner and drinks
with the dead

The bicyclers flew
through
five boroughs

I woke at noon,
relieved
The ghosts
had vanished

Cars cruised down
the highway
A horn blared
almost loud enough
to wake the zombies
inside

Helen Peterson

Marriage

Her father saw how proud she was--
a diamond crowned in gold
around her engagement finger.
Knowing his daughter
he gave a lot of land
for her and the women she loved
her so-called *lover* then
later called *partner*
now called *wife*
by Supreme Court order
and the land evolved into a wedding gift.

———

Temporary

Temporary is as airy
as the wings of a fairy
flaming into smoke.

Temporary is as airy
as a clear blue sky
trampled by rain.

Temporary is as airy
as sweeping sand Mandalas
made by Tibetan monks.

Su Polo

Pounding The Pavement
(For My Father)

Things remind me... Little things. Sometimes
The simplest of sounds or
Sights or a color of light
Nudges a thought.
The time of day casts your shadow.
A word or flavor on the tip of my
Tongue— suddenly you appear gazing
At me with your comments and the
Sound of your voice reminds my ears of
How much they miss you.
I want to drop down and pound
The pavement with my fists till it
Cracks open to release you and
Bring you up from the dust,
Bring you back to the world so
You can fix things again. And
I will stand there dutifully, happy
To hold a flashlight for you
Into the dark night
While you work.

Kelly J. Powell

Paris Is Burning
(After Suicide Bombings, November 2015)

Yes. its true. paris is burning!
And again, the whole world is watching.
And again, the whole world's enraged.

Tonight. the day after. its raining here.
People talking of inclusion—on a platform
Discouraged in much of the world— are being
Targeted in this our unique truly open forum.

And paris is still burning. leaders
Of the world's-a-stage are all
Checking in. heads of state of all colors
And kinds are checking in with compassion, concern.

For victims, their families, parisians
The french, europeans, bono for his fans, of course,
The performer.cancelling, protecting.

But Where Were All of Them
When Christine Died.
In Riverhead The Local News Reported The Accident.
A Traffic Incident. Single Mother, Unfortunate.

A PARAGRAPH.

Word On The Street Placed Her Back Out There
Near The Train Station. Back To Prostitution.
Back On Crack. A Deal Gone Wrong
Closed Her Arm In The Open Passenger Window
She'd Reached In To Get Back Her Money
They Dragged Her Along The Side Of The Car

UNTIL SHE DIED.

But paris is burning, again. cnn
Mentioned the frank family's visa rejected
In a climate such as this. already a day after.
Its raining today, right here.

Anoek van Praag

Early Morning

Sweet morning love
You sleep a crunched up face
your hand nearly in your mouth
the comfort of your body
Your busy mouth and head in quiet rest
My clothes drop on the floor
slide in the nest still warm
where lights were lit
from into each other
calm waters now
all rivers gone to sea

As if on cue your hand,
but not your body – motionless
crawls imperceptibly between my legs
Tenderly your fingers lie in active rest
My clitoris alert and shifting to my head
a little stirring now and then
the sun stopped moving watching us
all darkness gone
Your fingers reposition – almost not
to find the perfect spot
breathing soundless
the birth place
Universe stillness in the room
I am wide and open nerves
Sliding on thrills and wet
I am so glad I did go to sleep
This century of love

Ron Price

Unfinished

St. Sulpice

What better place to kneel
than the granite floor of this church
where all things bend

under the weight of what is
unfinished.
I must have come this way

by the moon's twenty-eight cobblestones.
I must have chosen the true way
of her body,

so much like the moon's.

The only other light here is an old woman
scarved in black,
kneeling before a lit votive candle,

her body
heavy, bent
over rosary beads,
wiping tears from her cheek.

My life amounted to a burden of words
in a few of her tears.

I entered this church having left a woman's
laughter, music
I held once with my whole body.

I came here,
having learned late of love's austerities,
the way an old woman's grief

echoes a young woman's laughter.

JD Rage

Bob Hart Is Gone

No, I don't think that's right
Bob is just over here in a slim slash of sunshine
creeping in my window
reminding me that I really should get out
of bed today. It might be nice to greet the
dawn before it disappears, like Bob
Yes, most of us can't see him anymore
even when we're looking straight in his face
where he's swirling in the beauty of the traffic
tip toeing through the flowers, marveling at
the lovely trees, now knowing their full beauty
no longer limited by living human eyes.

I hope that Bob is in a Bob Hart version of Heaven
and keeps sending us those notes on the universe
and every once in a while showing up at a reading
lending his inspiration, quoting his special
take on art and life for someone to pass on
to the wide world
I think we'll find Bob in the eternal movie house
in the museum and the gallery soaking in
the atmospheric melodies that he could always
hear.

But now he can see why he was enraptured
by songs and poems and paintings and he can
feel these miracles amplified by angelic voice
he can become part of their essence
at will, expanding the hearts and souls of all
who keep his memory from growing dim

Jill Rapaport

People Who Smile

People who smile are of another race. I have wondered about them many times.

I have been urged, myself, to smile, standing on a bridge. Wings raised, I have remained static, not smiling. I was oppressed by smiling people as I grew. Smiles burgeoned in sister, in mother, around the house amid the hedges. In school, I saw the smiles; saw the smiles in streets, cities, cars, beaches. I cut out the photo of a smiling beauty in a magazine, put it in a folder, kept it for years. I was riveted to smiling men, sometimes stunned with my face a mask. At jobs people not only smiled but demanded smile. Men on the street demanded smile. TV began to be filled with people who smile---if it hadn't always, and more and more it came to seem it had. The stores and their windows were filled with the people who smile. Smile as they pay for expensive food, clothes, boats. On top of these, more people who smiled lived grandly.

How dear the smile that eluded me and my mouth, for no reason I could grasp.

Janet Restino

I Hear The Land Crying Grandmother

I hear the land crying Grandmother
I hear the roots and the soil sobbing red tears
I see the worms turning Grandmother
and drowning in buckets of fear

I touch the bird's beak Grandmother
and it snipped me clean to the bone
I fear the earth is losing Grandmother
your tomatoes, your mint, your basil, your pears,
your figs, your corn
could be but a memory...could be but a memory

The worms oozed down Houston Street
under a raining reign
They were stepped on under our feet
they were squashed into the concrete
who will turn the soil?
who will feed the robin?
under a raining reign
Grandmother take away my pain

I burned a candle for you Grandmother...it burned so slowly
and with such a steady flame
I transformed my sadness and I promised in your name
to protect our Mother Earth...Mother Earth who gave us our birth

O beautiful for spacious skies...for amber waves......

What have they done to the skies?
sure makes me want to cover my eyes
what have they done to the soil?
sure makes my blood boil
what have they done to the grain?
they're messin with the food chain
makin the cows sick and insane
flushin Mother Nature down the drain
what have they done to the seeds?
Corporate greed's growin like weeds

GMO is not the way to sow
birds and butterflies meeting their demise
we got Cyclops frogs and more dead bees
Arctic meltdowns and rising seas
GMO is not the way to sow

What have they done to the sea?
it's been dumped with misery
what have they done to the birds?
I just can't find the words
drowning in oil slicks, the time bomb ticks and ticks
while Corporate rulers gets their kicks

What have they done to the rivers? ...it gives me the shivers
O the fish and the birds and the roaming herds
it's a crime, it's a sin, no one can win
what they've done to the soil...it makes my blood boil

Grandmother I hear the land crying crying crying
They wanna frack the land they should be banned
from rapin the Earth for all that she's worth
what they've done to the fish you never would wish
on your worst enemy...so much mercury
radioactive seaweed is not what nature needs

In the stillness and the shadow...in the silence and the flame
In the stillness and the shadow...in the silence and the flame
Grandmother I hear the land...I hear the land
crying crying crying...crying... crying... crying...

Barbara Rosenthal

At The Window, Fester, Snowy Morning After

I have kept you festering in my body. I have not washed you out.

It is dawn now, snowed last night still snowing so snowy out the window now and on the window ledge a light coat and beyond the window ledge the river so snowed into sky there is no river just the window *finestre fenster finêtre fin etre* the end of being you festering I can not harsh soap you out but must will let my own fluid fluency gently wash you through.

Here, catch! I throw you a snowball river to river, from me to you, west to east, the same direction as the wind.

Robert Roth

My Mother's Death: Three Months Later

In the cafe I look in the mirror. A gray fading face, its contours unchanged. On the cusp of looking old even to myself. As I walk down Bleecker St. a huge sadness comes over me. I remember walking down 8th St. three decades ago. The street almost deserted, except for a young teenage girl across the way. The light from the street lamp cast a soft glow over her. She had iron hooks for hands and she was just standing there crying, wiping her eyes with her arm. She looked so forlorn. I am so forlorn. The pain is overwhelming.

Thaddeus Rutkowski

Sea Crooner

When I get to the Indian Ocean, I don't expect to see much wildlife. But I'm going to have to be careful if I meet a dugong. I might be wading around, making my way through the sea grass, enjoying the bay and sky, when I might see a large shape in the water. The creature might have curves like a human, a female human, but it might be ten times the size. This woman-like monster might be swimming toward me gracefully, grazing on the sea grass, its bulk buoyant, its flippers waving. I'll have to tell myself not to get excited. It is not a siren, singing to me. Or is it? It certainly might be undulating, as if dancing, moving in a suggestive way. And if I put my ear to the water, I might hear a sort of bass, but no treble. Only bass—no treble—as the grass grazer approaches.

Is it a daughter of the river god, trying to lure me, as the god's daughters lured Odysseus in ancient times? The Greek captain heard their song, but he was fastened to the mast. His sailors abandoned ship to swim toward the divine sounds, but he couldn't leave. He had to stand there, beard out, eyes upward, and listen to the song.

Will this sea creature make me change course and founder on the rocks? I will have to hold tight to something, perhaps a pillar of coral, so I am not drawn toward that bass (no treble). The creature may be harmless. It may be no more than the largest herbivorous marine mammal there is, but I might feel its attraction. What if it approaches me and embraces me with its flippers and half-formed fluke? I don't want to be mowed over. What if it smothers me in skin that is so coarse it can't be pierced? I don't want to be trapped under tons of fun. It is time to get out of the dugong's way.

Ilka Scobie

On The Destruction Of The Seventh Century Winged Bull Of Assyria In Mosul, Iraq

The crowned head represents intelligence
No sapient shards penetrate the hatred
That shatters ancient artifacts

Horned caps were added to the secret tree of life as a good luck charm
Cursed luck creates decapitators, book burners, woman haters

Wings, a symbol of sovereign power
Soaring possibilities denied to freedom seeking women
imprisoned by ferocious fundamentalism

Words survive sledgehammers
O, for the cuneiform's curse:
Whoever would destroy the creation of my hands,
Let the Great Lord destroy his name and posterity on earth

Alan Semerdjian

Ferry Addict

Because the vacillation, ride and ride again, my sweet
indecision. Between what one never gets to

and everything one can't give up is an unfinished building
on the verge of irascible inclinations because the leaning

one way or another is never possible, not even close
to affected by wind or history, which is made up of a myriad

of these approximations inked in doubt and sullen fever
like the automaton that fans our short-lived travels into forever.

Be permanently inside where there is nothing but waiting
like the moments after an order at the take out spot

when a cigarette was a canon and the shot fired into the heart
of things to do. It is this precise kind of recollection

that I'm talking about. Go examine other cultures, learn
languages like love, explore the channel to your heart's content,

and, most of all, only urge and never get. Only sway
and never rock. Be in two places always and nowhere at once.

Brian Sheffield

My Body Tried To Start A Revolution

Let me ask you a question:

When was the last time you really let your eyeballs drop?
When was the last time you screwed open the top of your head
        and let your brain breathe?
When will all of...this...make sense?

My sober mind is a fountain of jewels.
My drunken mind is a fountain of wood.
My stoned mind is a stone.

The last time I let my eyeballs drop
My jewels turned into wood and
My body became a stone.

My fingers are architects.
My brain is a manual laborer
Organizing a strike against my fingers.

My vocal chords have armed themselves
Against the loudspeaker that
Calls from my stomach.

My feet are stolen property
That my legs reclaim with loud
Pamphlets and academic articles.

My text is no Pharmakon
Because it is already written
Within my soul.

I use my skin as a verb.
I use my genitals as punctuation.
All of my lovers are phrases and clauses.

I am neither I nor we;
I am undecidable.

Goodbye Plato—
You are no longer needed here.

Goodbye Ginsberg—
Your generation is becoming irrelevant.

Goodbye Writer—
Your words have already been stored
Within every database.

Soon, there will be too much language
To document in just another
Small press anthology.

Susan Sherman

Every Which Way

Imagine a globe spinning through space
You are standing in Canada   The stars are
singularly bright   You watch them in silence
You are standing in China   Bikers struggle
through crowded streets   pollution so dense
it obscures the light   You are standing in Spain
It is summer   The sun burns your flesh
as you reach toward your daughter's hand
You are standing in Africa   The Serengeti is quiet
Predators wait for night   You are standing in Antarctica
the sky dimming in preparation for winter's long sleep
You are standing at the North Pole   or in a big city
Calcutta perhaps   or Moscow Buenos Aires New York
You are standing in the suburbs   on the plains
on a island   Do you ever think it curious
no matter where you are   freed of gravity
you will fall into space   Perhaps even now you
slant at a ninety degree angle   or worse
with your head hanging permanently down
How athletic to be stretched out sideways
rigid as a board   What determination to remain
the wrong way round   the soles of your feet where
your head should be   Have you ever considered
how distorted our perception of who we are
how we are placed might be   when we are   all of us
standing   every which way but up

Dan Shot

What You Should Know

He's a man of mystery
     even to himself

Vertigo has been defeated

After all these years
     he still has a taste for Bukowski

The poem has trouble moving
     from point A to B to C
Baggage strewn upon a dirty floor
     in an unfinished room

He only drinks when he has to

Voices on the couch lost in 70's soul
     How did they ever get so old?

The unacknowledged King of Hoboken

Never thought he'd make it to thirty
     laughs about it now
Lush graveyards shrouded in memory
     seeking undiscovered countries

Like his sisters a by-product of Shoah

2034 steps to the train
     1642 steps from the train
measure fleeting thoughts' loss
     to time's widening gyre

Dim winter sun on Brooklyn beach
     the waves, the waves, Atlantic waves

Has heard the mermaids sing
     Doesn't care

The words do matter
     after she's gone.

Joanna Sit

Selfie

I smoke (but never in Chinatown)
I kiss (but never boys in Chinatown)
I curse (always in English, never in Chinese)
I sing Cantonese opera songs (but never at my mother's house
        and never to anyone)
I eat (sometimes to excess but never in a Chinese restaurant)
I drink (often in excess but never, not even beer, not one, in a
        Chinese restaurant. Unless that restaurant is in Thailand,
        but never if it's in Peru)
I weep (but never during disasters)
I smile (but never at a stranger. Especially a Chinese man)
I brag (but never to my family and never in Chinatown)
I fly into rages (but never at my family or those who tell me what
            to do)
I aim to please (always in excess)

But once the moon is lost
in its own blue and dark comes
too deep for any light to pass

When the griffin emerges from
the parabola of its trance and rakes
the night clouds over Cepheus
with scarlet claws and the sirocco
strips China to the bone

When no one's looking
to measure the distance
of what was there with what was
remembered in that twilight silence

Then, I forget myself
Then, I give myself up
Then, I walk into my cave

There, I seek release
There, I make peace
There, I forgive no one

There, I embrace insolence, pride, ingratitude
There, I rain down fire on continence
There, I absolve all desire
There, I dance with my monsters all night long

Miriam Stanley

Arthritis

Like flowers losing their petals,
or trees losing their leaves,
cartilage shrinks from the spine,
and now your posture crumbles,
hips twist,
shoulders jut;
there's the sheet of pain before sitting down.

Then there's the agony of getting up.

Millenials give up their seats, and suddenly
you are the Tin Man.

The stalled machine in the road;
the obstacle for everyone faster,
an annoyance for kids in a hurry,
a lump – a Glacial Lump.
You aren't strong, you get in everyone's way,
you are the weakest link in the chain
of humanity.

Your siblings have to help you.

...always so proud to live alone,
provide for yourself,
fix your own dinner,
even take care of pets,
bend down to clean the floor;
Now you're the constant patient
visiting the doctor's office.
And who will take care of you when you're worse?
Mishapen and childless,
whittled down to your last decade of life,
when action falls away
and you are weaker than fear:
who will help you now??

Alice B. Talkless

It Was The Year Of Holsters

There were a lot of people carrying.
They were open about it.
They had cell phones
guns,
babies
iPads or minis
sunglasses
and cold brews.

Belts were riveted
and full of holes, but filled–
every loop a buckle
as hook for holding
pills
mace
grenades
flint
tic–tacs
tinned fish
and other tools.

They were prepared, occupied
with ideas and fear,
hunters, who felt like prey.

J. M. Theisen de González

Crib Notes Of A Latent Bad Ass

Long ago, in Williamsburg, before the million dollar apartments and their trappings, a bar called the Right Bank existed, where it had art, music, and poetry. I "worked" there, splitting a reading series with Joanne. The night following one season's conclusion, I decided to see the Wild Bill show, and read once more. My bike had a flat tire, so this meant mass transit. After the show I hustled up to the Broadway / Bedford intersection, hoping to grab a bus; sputtering and wheezing its way back to Greenpoint. Aw, hell no-- there went the bus--EARLY! I stamped over to check the schedule- -nothing I needed. Whereupon, in the distance, I noticed a squad car, and further noticed its occupants noticing me. The car turned onto Bedford, executed a K turn, and backed up the wrong way to discuss things with me. As in, what was I doing there (waiting for a bus), did I know that this was a dangerous area (yes), and I should wait under a street light (I usually do). I turned my token over and over in my pocket. Officer Driver looked at me. I looked at him. Where do you live? Greenpoint. Get in.

Trust me when I say that if you haven't committed any societal transgressions, it's thrilling for your inner nine year old to ride in the back of a police cruiser. Like walking the walk in sensible shoes. We made small talk, as polite folks do. They inquired as to my point of departure and why I was there. The police seemed mildly curious to have a "local celeb" in the confines of the squad car. I was dropped off by the cops in front of mi casa, where much to my chagrin, my totally bitchin' moment was lost to the ages. No buttinsky neighbors in the windows from the elbows up, no corner beer boys tying one on. Not a soul. Greenpoint was a ghost town. Damn. I thanked them and lit upstairs. On Dominick the Rottweiler's evening constitutional, I recounted the tale. He seemed unfazed. Even so, I wouldn't trade my time of reflected bad-ass glory for a second, even if it wasn't strictly observed.

Zev Torres

Frenzy

In the flush of a night polished and gleaming
Like any night pulsating with a radiant sheen
Rushing around in an aspiring orbit
Broken free from the chain of days
They journey from party to event to bash to soiree
Taking their leave without fanfare or flair
Arrive not unnoticed at the next destination
Embrace toast dance until they're off again
To the next celestial gala or subterranean blowout
Their entourage click–clacking down the subway station stairs
Seven or eight of them – they started with a dozen lost a few
Either at the last venue or the one before that
No worries they'll all meet up again somewhere
Perhaps at the diner near twenty–third where they usually
converge
Those nights they take a turn around sunrise
Or they'll check in tomorrow afternoon or on Monday
Or on Tuesday or whenever someone will text or call
To catch up and fill in the blank spaces of the evening
Whom they met and how they got home
But 'til then the ones that are left will hold the train doors open
Or they will stuff themselves into a taxi
Or haggle with a limo driver or
Wait for their rideshare to show up
Or just walk from one place to another
In their gowns and stiletto heels
While the frenzied atoms of the night
Cavort on their skin.

Bruce Weber

A Strange Day

it was a strange day. tulips blossomed
as tall as midtown skyscrapers. denice
cried in a towel. the rock on the shelf
glowed mischievously. every bar room
leaned to the left. blue clouds walked
into the subway station and purred like
kittens. we wandered aimlessly through
tunnels looking for a silver lining.

it was a strange day. harvey raised a
drink and praised the sea and sky and
sun. he became consumed by the letter
s. tieing it around his throat like a scarf.
shamelessly plugging samantha's new
book. sandra's unhooked bra. susie's
invisible playmate. i stood in the sun
and waved at an airplane. i took out
my weasel and stared off to mars.
i rubbed the gleaming ball and promised
i would remain a virgin till man walked
on mars. all the s's in the universe fell
asleep and i was alone. finally, gloriously.
alone.

it was an aluminum day. a steel day. a
lead day. all the metal collectors were
happy. they jumped up like a mexican
bean dance. they galloped across the
city like a herd of happy horses. they
filled the lanes of the highways with
throbbing glee. they portrayed them—
selves as free of porcelain. bereft of
ivory. devoid of makeshift stainless
steel epiphanies.

it was a narrow day. a day difficult to
fit between sentences. a day thin as
forgetfulness. a day hiding under the
basement boiler. a day hibernating
in memory. a day split asunder.
disappearing down a manhole.
betraying sunlight. a day fizzling away
to nothing. a day like any other apocalypse.

Jeffrey Cyphers Wright

Staggering Love

How cheap is blood, it runs in the streets
How naked is aggression
Selling its garments to buy a weapon
How high is the high ground
When the flood is a sea of faces
When a sandstorm fills the sandbox
How shall we all get along
Relics of the bone codex
The days grow shorter, while night
Grows a long beard
We are all "bull" fighters now
Prisoners of staged danger
Don't point a finger at your neighbors
Slay stray dragons with staggering love

Anton Yakovlev

The Apprehension

"Oh yes, a lot of headless chickens in this town!"
whispered a fast-track businessman on the subway
to his friend before
he pushed me out of the way
with a polite "Thank you" at 14th Street.

From inside the train, I watched them
dominate the exit turnstiles,
while all around them oversize flightless birds
with bloody holes in place of their necks
stumbled awkwardly into each other,
falling off the platform by the dozen.

Still a long ride before I'd reach Coney Island—
and all I saw was a whole lot of dead chickens walking.

I had to find a way to see them differently.
So I pictured them as dinosaurs—
green, and tan, and magenta, and militant.

A dinosaur brushed a model airplane against me.

But it was a fox, not a dinosaur,
that accused me of being too in his face
then threatened me with a bag full of landscape paintings.

From the bridge, I saw a sickly zebra
drive a motorboat across the East River
then dump a lion's body into the currents.

In the second-floor window of a steakhouse,
a pale hyena was staring at a TV.

A dead shark floated in formaldehyde,
making a powerful statement.

I exited the train at the last station,
walked down a staircase built of musical chairs.

The way to the ocean was full of carnivorous plants—
it took all my skill to survive their petals.

I stood in front of a giant python covered in little carts,
talking politics with an old friend I'd run into,
amazed at never having noticed before
that he was actually a rhino.

Robots were picking currants.
A fried dough saleswolf was devouring a skunk's tail.
A kangaroo shoved babies into herself.

The monkfish, the crows, the meerkats, the tics, the doe,
the professional clenchers of teeth, the doomed and the graceless,
the elephants, the mutants, the Firebird's ashes,
the horned one, the liquid, the apparitions, the plasma dogs
shrieked, shrugged, shook, dashed, wailed, waltzed on the edge
of the ocean—

then a hand tugged at my sleeve,
and the menagerie went
silent.

Susan L. Yung

Inequities

(I am getting' such segregationistic emails. Ever since NYC has
ethnic museums, ethnic, visible ethnic community centers,
ethnic theater centers for ethnic performances... Equality means
something else & probably writers are the only ones perceiving
the inequities. — July 13, 2015)

Nobody bothers about
the deaths of Black men
killed by Cops
Only Black people
in Amerika

Nobody bothers about
White people making
others homeless
or losing jobs
or small businesses
or making a pack
with the capitalist
devil
but rather
what is love anyways?
to honor & support
til death do us part
in God's eyes?

NOT
It is get a divorce and
let him pay
the alimony
she can keep the house
"I'm movin' to
another town.", he says

If not married
then he expects
you to be his equal.
He pays

You pay
"You hold up half the sky", Mao said.
& China believes it
except
you must bear a son

Here, women
only makes
70% to your dollar.

In other words,
A woman college graduate
will earn
a million dollars
less than a man.
So men should pay
our tips,
& taxes on
"her" behalf.

Angelo Zeolla

Mondrayork

Saturday night
Ngope ru mol a Mondragone
Emcees rhyme these versi immacolati
defaming cosidetti sfigati
For even picking up a microphone,

Motorini fly by purring in the distance
and the skaters are the shit
nel stare a mostro con i loro trick
e per la strada si vedono
passare guaglioncelle,
con dei loro sguardi da stelle,
che vanno di moda vestite tutto chic.

And one cat over by the kebab
truck sheepishly asks another:

O Fra' ma 'a canna 'a tieni?

Other cat si esce fore' con un pezzo—
tipo un mattone,
a fat chunk he copped
Over a ru terz' munn'
Si fa sta pinta,
it gets sparked
And soon ognuno
se ne va
A chiedere:

Ma stu tir' se po' fa' o no?

A red moon draped in malinconia peeks down
at streets that stay littered con spazzatura

As i caramba drive by
with their ice grills that
make blood chill,
cio'e' fanno paura,

the perfume of tainted Mediterranean air
lingers thru the scene
and nocturnal writers throw up a wild style piece
that declares to new arrivals
that peep every street sign,
in wonder,
as they bewilderedly walk:

Benvenuti a MondraYork!

APPENDIX

CONTRIBUTOR BIOGRAPHIES

Austin Alexis

Austin Alexis received the **Madgett Poetry Award** for **Privacy Issues** (2014), and is also the author of two chapbooks: **Lovers and Drag Queens** (2007) and **For Lincoln & Other Poems** (2010). He has fiction and poetry published or forthcoming in **J Journal, Home Planet News, The Ledge, The Journal** and in the anthology **Rabbit Ears: TV Poems**.

Joel Allegretti

Joel Allegretti is the author of five collections of poetry. His second collection, **Father Silicon** (**The Poet's Press**, 2006), was selected by **The Kansas City Star** as one of 100 Noteworthy Books of 2006. He is the editor of **Rabbit Ears: TV Poems** (**NYQ Books**, 2015), the first anthology of poetry about the mass medium.

Amber

The cornucopia fruit and vegetable lady, from apple to zucchini. Poems published, performed, taped, translated. Hosted monthly office poetry events. Amber illuminates.

Maria Aponte

Maria Aponte – Community Arts Activist / Educator. Her work focuses on growing in NYC's El Barrio and the Puerto Rican woman's experience. She has been featured on Bronx Net, NBC Latino and performs her work locally and nationally. In May 2013, her book **Transitions of a Nuyorican Cinderella** won 2nd Place for Best Poetry in English at the **International Latino Book Awards**.

Madeline Artenberg

Madeline Artenberg's poetry has appeared in many print and online publications, such as **Vernacular and Rattle**. She won Lyric Recovery and Poetry Forum prizes and was semi-finalist in the 2005 contest of **Margie, The American Journal of Poetry**. Her work often touches on Jewish and New York City themes. **The Old In-and-Out**, a play based on her poetry and that of Karen Hildebrand, directed by Kat Georges, garnered raves in June, 2013.

Ayres

Ayres read for the first time @ the Annual Alternative New Year's Day reading 2(-) years ago. "I Am a Flim-Maker (sic)!" (1994–2015) appears in print for the first time! In 2016, Ayres, his middle name, will have a 4–6 week retrospective (Wallpaper & Beyond) with 2 (film) screenings + a 200–300(-) page book @ Printed Matter.

Gabriella M. Belfiglio

Gabriella M. Belfiglio lives in Brooklyn, NY. She teaches self-defense, conflict resolution, karate, and tai chi. Gabriella won second place in the 2014 **W.B. Yeats Poetry Contest**. Gabriella's work has been published in many anthologies and journals including **VIA, Literary Mama, The Avocet, The Potomac Review, Lambda Literary Review**. Her website is www.gabriellabelfiglio.info

Patricia Carragon

Patricia Carragon loves cupcakes, chocolate, cats, haiku, and Brooklyn. Her publication credits include **BigCityLit**, **Boog City**, **Clockwise Cat**, **Yellow Chair Review**, and others. Her latest chapbook, **The Cupcake Chronicles**, is forthcoming from **Poets Wear Prada**, winter 2015. She hosts the Brooklyn-based **Brownstone Poets** and is the editor-in-chief of its annual anthology.

Tina Chan

Tina Chan is a lively poet whose writing style is a poetic puzzle. She believes words extracted from the heart are to be made memorable.

Steve Dalachinsky

Poet / collagist Steve Dalachinsky was born in Brooklyn after the last big war and has managed to survive lots of little wars. His book **The Final Nite (Ugly Duckling Presse)** won the **PEN Oakland National Book Award**. His most recent books are **Fools Gold** (2014 **Feral Press**), **A Superintendent's Eyes** (revised and expanded 2013 / 14 – **Unbearable / Autonomedia**) and **Flying Home**, a collaboration with German visual artist Sig Bang Schmidt (**Paris Lit Up Press** 2015). His latest CD is **The Fallout of Dreams** with Dave Liebman and Richie Beirach (**Roguart** 2014). He is a 2014 recipient of a **Chevalier D' le Ordre des Artes et Lettres**. He is also a 2015 Pushcart Prize nominee.

Vivian Demuth

Vivian Demuth's poetry book, **Fire Watcher**, published by **Guernica Editions** highlights "lively eco-poems with an exquisite eye for detail and a profound concern for the larger environmental picture." Vivian is also the author of two novels, **Bear War-den**, and E**yes of the Forest**. Her writing has been published in journals / anthologies in Canada, the USA, Mexico, and Europe.

Pete Dolack

Pete Dolack is an activist, essayist, poet and photographer who tries to keep juggling all these balls but, alas, keeps dropping some of them. Pete currently writes about the economic and environmental crisis and what a better world might look like on the **Systemic Disorder** blog, and his book **It's Not Over: Learning From the Socialist Experiment** will be published in February.

Gabriel Don

Gabriel Don received her MFA in creative writing at The New School, where she worked as the Reading Series and Chapbook Competition Coordinator. Her writing has appeared in **The Brooklyn Rail**, **The Sydney Morning Herald**, **Westerly**, **Mascara Literary Review**, **Transtierros** (translated into Spanish), **Gargoyle 62**, **LiveMag! 12**, **Gainsayer and Three Rooms Press**, **MAINTENANT 9**. She currently teaches writing at BMCC.

Akeem K. Duncan

Hailing from the southeast section of the Bronx, Akeem K. Duncan is inspired by an off-kilter harmony of love, drugs, instinct and generational existentialism. His work usually comes in the form of what he affectionately refers to as "receipt poems," brief but sweet excerpts scribbled on the back of pieces of paper. He is also an entrepreneur, an aspiring curator and currently heads a grassroots art magazine titled **Quiet Lunch**.

Bill Evans

Bill Evans' book of poems, **Modern Adventures**, was published by **Spuyten Duyvil** press in 2014. He's lives in the East Village, almost around the corner.

Cheryl J. Fish

Cheryl J. Fish's short fiction has been featured in **Liars League NYC** and she was a finalist for **L Magazine's Literary Upstart** search for pocket fiction. Her most recent poetry chapbook is **Make It Funny, Make it Last** (#171, **Belladonna Chaplets**, 2014). Her poetry has appeared in **The Bloomsbury Anthology of Contemporary Jewish American Poetry**; **Far from the Centers of Ambition: The Legacy of Black Mountain College**; Terrain. org; **New American Writing**; **Talisman**; **Kudzu House Review**, and **Volt**.

Bryan Fox

Bryan Cornel Fox is a New York poet who loves to box and has performed poetry around the city at places such as Nuyorican Poets' Café, GLBT Center, Word at 4F, and the Bowery Poetry Club.

Armando Jaramillo Garcia

Armando Jaramillo Garcia was born in Colombia, South America and raised in New York City. He attended Hunter College and currently works as a photo industry professional at a science and medical agency. He has published recently in **Prelude**, **Horse Less Review**, **ThoseThatThis**, **TYPO**, **The Opiate**, **Jerkpoet**, **Kentucky Review** and others.

Robert Gibbons

Robert Gibbons is a poet living in New York City- Brooklyn. With more than 10 years under his belt in search of his muse, It could be Langston, or Baldwin, or Frank Ohara or Baraka, but it is the muse goddamit that he is search of. The publishing credit are too numerous and lengthy to enumerate for he likes compression. He like the brevitas with long enunciations and chants. He likes to worship the ancestors and Cleo, the goddess of History. There is no telling what will be found on his next elephant hunt. Maybe he will find his lost friend Nomusa with her amphora. Robert's first collection was published in 2012 by **Three Rooms Press**, entitled **Close to the Tree.**

Russ Green

Russ Green is a Graduate of Hofstra University. He is co-editor at **Great Weather for Media**, runs readings on Long Island and has a book called **Gimme Back My Radio**. He can be found in the mountains with crazy artist friends or roaming the docks of Port Jefferson at night with his tuxedo cat.

Antonia Greenberg

I'm 17 and currently a junior at Beacon H.S., NYC. Been writing since I discovered William Carlos Williams in the 6th grade and realized the notes I taped to the refrigerator constituted poetry! I've taken courses at Columbia in creative writing and currently write songs and poetry with my band, and when I'm most particularly inspired on the downtown 1 train. Writing for me has expressed the words I've only been able to say with a pen, and will hopefully always remain a source of happiness in my life.

Bob Heman

Bob Heman has edited **CLWN WR** (formerly **Clown War**) since 1972. His collages have appeared recently in **Caliban** online, **Right Hand Pointing**, **Skidrow Penthouse**, **Fell Swoop** and **Clockwise Cat**. During the late 1970s he was an artist-in-residence at the Brooklyn Museum.

Aimee Herman

Aimee Herman is the author of two full-length books of poems and teaches writing in the Bronx.

Roxanne Hoffman

Roxanne Hoffman worked on Wall Street, now answers a patient hotline. Her words can be found in cyberspace, set to music, on the silver screen, and in print. She and Jack Cooper run **Poets Wear Prada**. Her elegiac poem "In Loving Memory," illustrated by Edward Odwitt, was released as a chapbook in 2011.

Kate Irving

Kate Irving's poems have appeared in, among others, BigCityLit. com, **qaartsiluni**, and **Press 1**. Her chapbook, "Raising the Arsonist's Daughter from the Dead" was published by **Finishing Line Press** in 2014. She grew up in NYC and is grateful for that unique education.

Evie Ivy

Evie Ivy is a dancer / poet in the NYC poetry circuit. She hosts one of the longest running poetry series, **The Green Pavilion Poetry Event** in Brooklyn. Her latest book out is "Living in 12-Tone... and other poetic forms."

C. D. Johnson

C. D. (Seedy) Johnson: Former web developer, webmaster, and I.T. Director for CEO Clubs International, Inc. Currently, a freelance web, software, and digital publishing consultant. Holds an M.A. in analytic philosophy and logic theory and a B.S. in computer science. Has taught religious instruction in Sanatana Dharma and Shaktism, as well as Advaita Vedanta. Current projects include an 800 page magnus opus on theology and mysticism that no one will want to read, research into Indian Nyaya logic, and a conlang (constructed language) project. C. D. is the graphics artist for the Alternative New Year's Day Spoken Word / Performance Extravaganza. As editor-in-chief of Rogue Scholars Press, he is the editor and publisher of the ANYDSWPE annual anthology. He likes to anger people in his spare time.

Boni Joi

Boni Joi was born in North Miami Beach, Florida, raised in New Jersey and discovered her lost lineage in Salem, Massachusetts. She has a MFA in poetry from Columbia University and has read and performed her poems at numerous venues in New Jersey, New York and elsewhere including Switzerland, Canada, and England. Her poems have appeared in **Arabella, Long Shot, Boog City Reader, Big Hammer, Lungfull!, The Brooklyn Rail** and many other journals. Her first collection of poetry, **Before During or After Rainstorms**, was published in 2012. Boston Review says: "Armed with an eye for the particular and a knack for gentle satire, Joi writes from the front lines of a doomed fight for America's spirit, but does so with a bright infectious gusto." Boni is an editor and project manager for **Black Square Editions**, a small poetry press and has designed their website: www.blacksquareeditions.org. She works a photograph and reference archivist and lives with musical chef Tobi Joi in Brooklyn.

Tobi Joi

Tobi Joi is one of Switzerland's premier rockers. Known for his bass guitar and trumpet playing skills in bands such as **Lobster, The Flying Shrimps, Take A Virgin, Moped Lads, Steven's Nude Club & the Nude Horns, Sylvia Juncosa Band**, and Switzerland's only Mod band **The Reaction** and many more. Audiences experience stoner-rock anthems and heavy psychedelic bass and drum symphonies that meander to a fully amplified crawl.

Larry Jones

Larry Jones was the co-producer along with Bruce Weber of the first five **ANYDSWPE** events at Café Nico, his loft apartment / performance venue one flight above the Pyramid Club on Avenue A. An Associate of the **Academy of American Poets**, his work has appeared in many literary magazines and anthologies. He teaches literature and creative writing to gifted and talented youth at Hofstra University.

Meg Kaizu

Meg Kaizu has lived in Tokyo, Moscow, and NYC, contributing articles for magazines such as **Tokyo Art Beat, PingMag, Whitehot Magazine, Being A Broad, Metropolis**, and **New York Art Beat**. Her paintings, prose and poetry have appeared in **KD-Magazine, Avenue, Off-Yellow**, and **Otter Magazine**. She studied art at the University of Oregon and the Art Students League of New York.

Ron Kolm

Ron Kolm is a contributing editor of **Sensitive Skin magazine**. He's the author of **The Plastic Factory, Divine Comedy** and **Suburban Ambush**. A collection of stories, **Duke & Jill**, has just been published by **Unknown Press**. He's had work in **Live Mag!, The Otter** and **The Outlaw Bible of American Poetry**. Ron's papers were purchased by the New York University library.

Ptr Kozlowski

Ptr Kozlowski has been a taxi driver, a deliveryman, a poet and a printer, singer–songwriter and guitarist. He likes to draw upon his experience to bring a musical perspective to the spoken word. He's been published in **Hobo Jungle** and **Curare**, in anthologies of **Brownstone Poets** and **Great Weather for Media**; and performed at CBGB's and The SIN Club, Bowery Poetry Club and ABC No Rio, Cornelia Street Cafe, the Saturn Series, Yippie Museum Cafe and Barnes and Noble Park Slope, among others. "Where's My Poem" was in **Stained Sheets** for Winter 2009.

Wayne Kral

Wayne Kral has lived in the Lower East Side for the last 26 years. He is an artist, writer and a musician, in that order.

Jane LeCroy

Jane LeCroy: (**Sister Spit**, **Vitapup**, **Nu Voices**, **Ohmslice**, **Transmitting**) fronts the avant-pop-post-punk band, **The Icebergs**, with Tom Abbs and David Rogers-Berry. **Three Rooms Press** published her multimedia book of lyrical poems,"Signature Play"

Linda Lerner

Yes, the Ducks Were Real, was published by **NYQ Books** (Feb. 2015) as was my previous collection, **Takes Guts and Years Sometimes**. A chapbook of poems inspired by nursery rhymes, illustrated by Donna Kerness, **Ding Dong the Bell Pussy in the Well** was published by **Lummox Press**, Feb. 2014. I've been nominated three times for a Pushcart Prize.

Phillip X Levine

Phillip X Levine lives near Woostock, NY and is approximately an actor, poet, poetry editor for **Chronogram** magazine and president of the Woodstock Poetry Society.

Steven T. Licardi

Steven T. Licardi is an author, spoken word poet, actor, motivational speaker, and activist who performs prominently across Long Island and Manhattan. Steven uses his work to engage in political discourse in order to positively affect society and culture. Steven believes in the power of art to teach love, altruism, selflessness, and compassion. For more, visit his website: TheSvenBo.com

Tsaurah Litzky

Tsaurah Litzky, a widely published poet, also writes fiction, memoir, erotica, plays and commentary. **Baby On The Water** (**Long Shot Press**) and **Cleaning The Duck (Bowery Books**) are her poetry collections. The most recent of her twelve chapbooks is **Jerry in the Bardo (NightBallet Press)**. She curates The Resistance reading series at Gallery Gaia, Vinegar Hill, Brooklyn.

Veronica Liu

Veronica Liu's writing, comics, photography, and silkscreen prints have been published in **Broken Pencil**, **Quick Fiction**, **We'll Never Have Paris**, and other publications, and she has received artist grants from Northern Manhattan Arts Alliance, Manhattan Community Arts Fund, Citizens Committee, and the Goodman Fund. She is founder of Word Up Community Bookshop, a volunteer-run, multilingual community space in Washington Heights.

Ellen Aug Lytle

This may be the year, 2016, I finally either finish my novel or chop it into short stories; probably the latter! Still teaching for **Poets and Writers** and trying my damnedest to help the world some and especially animals.

Nancy Mercado

Nancy Mercado is the editor of **The Nuyorican Women Writers Anthology** published by the **Center for Puerto Rican Studies** at Hunter College, CUNY. Featured on National Public Radio's **The Talk of the Nation** and the PBS NewsHour Special: **America Remembers 9/11**, she has authored a poetry collection: **It Concerns the Madness**, 7 theater plays and edited **If The World Were Mind: A Children's Anthology**.

Marlene Nadle

Marlene Nadle is a former reporter for **The Village Voice** and writer on politics and the arts.

Uche Nduka

Uche Nduka is a Nigerian–American poet, essayist, lyricist & dancer. He is the author of ten volumes of poems of which the most recent are **If Only The Night**, **eel on reef**, **Ijele**, **Nine East**. Some of his writings have been translated into German, Dutch, Finnish, Spanish, Italian, Serbo-Croat. He presently lives in New York City and teaches at Queens College.

Ngoma

Ngoma is a performance poet, multi-instrumentalist, singer / songwriter and paradigm shifter, who for over 40 years has used culture as a tool to raise socio-political and spiritual consciousness through work that encourages critical thought. Ngoma weaves poetry and song that raises contradictions and searches for a solution to a just and peaceful world.

Bri Onishea

Bri Onishea is a want-to-be-gypsy, an ardent lover of words, and an amateur in many things. A curious creature by nature, she hopes to pursue a lifetime of art and learning.

Jane Ormerod

Jane Ormerod is the author of **Welcome to the Museum of Cattle** (**Three Rooms Press**, 2012), **Recreational Vehicles on Fire** (**Three Rooms Press**, 2009), and the chapbook **11 Films** (**Modern Metrics / EXOT Books**, 2008). Born on the south coast of England, Jane now lives in New York City and performs extensively across the United States and beyond. She is a founding editor at **Great Weather for Media**.

Yuko Otomo

Yuko Otomo. Japanese origin. A bilingual (Japanese & English) poet & a visual artist. She also writes haiku, art criticism & essays. She has read in St. Mark's Poetry Project, Tribes, Bowery Poetry Club, ABC No Rio, La Mama, The Living Theatre, PS1, MoMA, The Queens Museum, etc & in Japan, France & Germany. Her publication includes "Garden: Selected Haiku" (**Beehive Press**), "A Sunday Afternoon on the Isle of Museum" (**Propaganda Press**), "PINK" (**Sisyphus Press**), "Small Poems" (**Ugly Duckling Presse**), "The Hand of The Poet" (**UDP**), "STUDY & Other Poems on Art" (**UDP**) & "Elements" (**the Feral Press**). She exhibited her artwork at Court House Gallery @ Anthology Film Archives, Tribes Gallery & Vision Festival, etc. She is a contributing writer for a collective art critical forum www.Arteidolia.com currently. Yuko is a 2015 Pushcart Prize nominee.

Amy Ouzoonian

Amy Ouzoonian is an artist, yoga teacher, dancer and member of the band **Expat**. She lives and creates in Phoenix, AZ.

Mireya Perez

Mireya Perez's poetry searches for that "other voice" breaking through entrapment and oppression, the fragile markers to unearth more hidden voices. Her work appears in **Revista del Hada, Caribbean Review, Americas Review, Diosas en Bronce: Anthology of Colombian Women Writers, IRP Voices**, among others.

Puma Perl

Puma Perl is a performer, producer, and a widely published poet / writer. She's the author of two chapbooks, **Belinda and Her Friends** and **Ruby True**, and two full-length collections, **knuckle tattoos** and **Retrograde**. As Puma Perl and Friends, she performs with some of NYC's best musicians and merges poetry with rock 'n roll. She is a regular contributor to **The Villager**.

Helen Peterson

Helen Peterson, M.A., a Cuba-native, performs her poems with castanets. Awards from **Mobius, The Poetry Magazine**; **Pen and Brush**; Geraldine R. Dodge Foundation among others Publications: **Mobius, The Poetry Magazine**; **U.S. 1 Worksheet**; **Avocet**; among others REVIEW: Experience...magic and genius of Helen's [poetry]...heart and soul.--Ellen Gilmer, **IPAIMPRESS**.

Su Polo

Native New Yorker, Su Polo is a writer of poems and stories, singer / songwriter with guitar / dulcimer, Jazz vocalist and graphic artist. Her book, **Turning Stones**, is at St. Marks Books. She's founder / host of Saturn Series poetry reading in its 22nd year every Monday night, NYC. For 10 years Su designed the stage for the Alternative New Years Day Poetry Extravaganza. http://www.supolo.com

Kelly J. Powell

Kelly J. Powell is a poet from Long Island.

Ron Price

Ron Price is a Teaching Artist at Juilliard. His most recent collection is **A True Account of the Failure of Bodies to Adequately Burn**.

JD Rage

JD Rage writes poetry and novels, paints and takes photographs and often appears in strange places for no good reason. When able, she publishes **CURARE** magazine and runs **Venom Press**.

Jill Rapaport

Jill Rapaport's collection of fiction, **Duchamp et Moi and Other Stories**, was published by **Fly by Night Press** / **A Gathering of the Tribes** in 2014.

Janet Restino

Janet Restino. multimedia artist. Philly roots & NYC streets. formally trained sculptor. eyes & hands. finding voice lifelong journey. funded by **Poets & Writers**, found on Youtube, etc. hosted own radio show **Heart & Soul**, recorded **Love Poems & Fast Songs**. Coming soon...**Canary in a Coal Mine**, stories, poems, songs. Art for the people: www.cafepress.com/ janetsarthouse & www.janetrestino.com

Barbara Rosenthal

Barbara Rosenthal is a NY Media Poet whose works explore intense human relationships. She belongs to the Unbearables Collective. **VSW Press** published four of her books. Her new novel, **WISH FOR AMNESIA** is just out from **Deadly Chaps Press**. She's read at Cornelia, Parkside, Bowery, etc, been published in **LiveMag**, **MacGuffin**, **Assembling**; taught at CUNY; and writes reviews for **Ragazine**.

Thaddeus Rutkowski

Thaddeus Rutkowski is the author of the books **Violent Outbursts, Haywire, Tetched and Roughhouse. Haywire** won the Members' Choice Award, given by the Asian American Writers' Workshop. He teaches at Medgar Evers College and the Writer's Voice of the West Side YMCA in New York. He received a fiction fellowship from the New York Foundation for the Arts.

Ilka Scobie

Ilka Scobie is a native New Yorker. Her recent poems appear in **Glitter Mob**, **Urban Graffiti** and here / there. She is a deputy editor of **Live Mag**. She writes about contemporary art for **London ArtLyst** and **White Hot**. She co-curated a group show Art Am 3 in Soncino, Italy with her husband, Luigi Cazzaniga.

Alan Semerdjian

Writer, musician, and educator Alan Semerdjian's poems and essays have appeared in print and online publications and anthologies including **Adbusters**, **Diagram**, and **Brooklyn Rail**. He released a chapbook of poems called **An Improvised Device** (**Lock n Load Press**) in 2005 and his first full-length book **In the Architecture of Bone** (**GenPop Books**) in 2009.

Brian Sheffield

Brian Sheffield is a poet from California living in Brooklyn and is pretty sure that he takes himself way too seriously. He is immature and talks about himself way too much. He has taught in various public school and university classrooms and has been published a few anthologies, journals, and zines. Oh yeah, he also has chapbooks.

Susan Sherman

Susan Sherman: Most recent books are **Nirvana on Ninth Street**, short Fiction with photos by Colleen McKay and **An Afterward by Rona L. Holub** (**Wings Press**, Fall, 2014); **The Light that Puts an End to Dreams: New and Selected Poems** (**Wings Press**, 2012); **America's Child: A Woman's Journey through the Radical Sixties**, a memoir (**Curbstone / Northwestern University Press**, 2007). She has survived living and writing in the East Village / Lower East Side for over fifty years.

Dan Shot

Dan Shot lives in Hoboken. He is doomed to write prosaic poetry and poetic prose. He very much agrees with Ralph Ellison that "life is to be lived, not controlled, and humanity is won by continuing to play in face of certain defeat."

Joanna Sit

Joanna Sit was born in China and grew up in on the Lower East Side. She is the author of two books of poetry: **My Last Century** and **In Thailand with the Apostles**, and she is working on an oral history about Cantonese Opera and New York Chinese immigrants.

Alice B. Talkless

Alice B. Talkless is Ronna Lebo, a poet, musician and painter who has performed in the NY scene for over twenty years. She is co-founder of **Black Square Editions**, a non-profit press for poetry and art. She is also co-founder of Reservoir Art Space in Ridgewood, Queens, which includes private studios and an experimental gallery for visual arts.

J. M. Theisen de González

JM Theisen de González received her first rejection letter at age 9 from **Reader's Digest** when her proud Gramps submitted a homework assignment about Lucky the hamster. Previous publications / venues: "The Curse", "Pink Pages", East Village Eye, "Waterfront Week" (columnist), "Estrellas" , Knitting Factory, Nuyorican Cafe, McManus Cafe, Pussycat Lounge, Right Bank, Charleston; in Spain: La Llotja, Hotel Colón, Bar Babia.

Zev Torres

Zev Torres' poetry has appeared in numerous print and on-line publications including the previous **ANYDSWPE** anthologies and the 2010-2015 **Brownstone Poets Anthologies**. In addition to featuring at poetry readings throughout New York, Zev hosts the Skewered Syntax Poetry Crawls and Make Music New York's annual Spoken Word Spectacular.

Bruce Weber

Bruce Weber is the author of five published books of poetry, including **The Break-up of My First Marriage (Rogue Scholars Press)**, and is the producer of the long running Alternative New Year's Day Spoken Word / Performance Extravaganza. By day, Bruce is Curator of **Paintings & Sculpture** at the Museum of the City of New York.

Jeffrey Cyphers Wright

Jeffrey Cyphers Wright is a poet, artist, critic, eco-activist, and impresario. He also edits and publishes **Live Mag!** His 13th book is a manifesto titled **Party Everywhere**. Wright's poem "Staggering Love" originally appeared in New Verse News.

Anton Yakovlev

Anton Yakovlev, originally from Moscow, Russia, is the author of chapbooks **Neptune Court** and **The Ghost of Grant Wood**. He has also directed several short films.

Susan L. Yung

Domestic-violence; misogynist-hater; anti-racist; democractic-anarchist; ghettoe-girl; Chinatown-Harlem; East Village-West Village; homesteader-gentrifier; yuppie-squatter; homeless-sheltered; American-Asian; World-Traveller; Adventress-Common-Law-Wife; Photographer-Videographer; Martial-Fine-Artist; Musician-Drummer; Artist-Scientist; Geologist-Librarian; Mathematician-Designer; Collector-Exhibitionist; Buyer-Seller; Cook-Politician; Migrant-worker; Independent-Dependent; Pacifist-Activist.

•

ROGUE SCHOLARS
Press

For General Information, go to:

http://www.roguescholars.com

For more information or a price quote for our
book design and editing services, contact:

publisher@roguescholars.com

•

Other ANYDSWPE Volumes From Rogue Scholars Press:

Estrellas En El Fuego (Stars In The Fire) - 2014
ISBN: 978-0-9840982-9-3

Shadow Of The Geode (Sombra Del Geode) - 2015
ISBN: 978-0-9840982-2-4 (2nd Edition)

•

22 Years!

The Alternative New Year's Day Spoken Word / Performance Extravaganza!

http://alternativenyd.org

www.ingramcontent.com/pod-product-compliance
Lightning Source LLC
LaVergne TN
LVHW041156080426
835511LV00006B/620